The Journey
from
Anxiety to Peace

Practical Steps to Handle Fear,
Embrace Struggle, and Eliminate Worry
to Become Happy and Free

Jean Walters

The Journey from Anxiety to Peace: Practical Steps to Handle Fear, Embrace Struggle, and Eliminate Worry to Become Happy and Free

Jean Walters
Inner Connections

Published by Inner Connections, St. Louis, Mo.

Copyright@2020 by Jean Walters
All Rights Reserved

No part of this book may be reproduced without written permission from the publisher or copyright holders, except for a reviewer who may quote brief passages in a review; nor may any part of this book be reproduced, stored in a retrieval system, or transmitted in any form or by any means electronic, mechanical, photocopying, recording or other, without written permission from the publisher or copyright holders.

Editor: Anne Cote, acote636@gmail.com
Cover design: Davis Creative. Davis Creative.com
Interior Design: Jen Henderson, Wildwordsformatting.com

Library of Congress Cataloging-in-Publication Data
Library of Congress Control Number: 1-8517547921

Designed and formatted in the United States of America

Welcome Reader

Thank you for your support in purchasing this book. It is my great joy to share this information with you that you may live an exalted life of freedom and peace.

Please check out my video library on youtube.com that promises to instruct you in universal laws, meditation techniques, and personal empowerment. By understanding these principles and applying them to your life, you become the master of your destiny and you open to greater and greater possibilities. May you be enriched.

About Jean Walters

Jean Walters is a Saint Louis based teacher of self-empowerment principles for forty years. She has studied metaphysics extensively and applies universal principles to every area of her life. She has written for major newspapers and publications. Her articles have appeared all over the United States. Her syndicated radio show, Positive Moments, was broadcast in 110 markets nationally.

Jean's passion is helping people recognize their innate power and place in the universe as divine beings and to live fully from that knowing. Her specialties are transformational coaching, metaphysics, dream interpretation, Akashic readings (over 35,000 given), metaphysics and public speaking.

Table of Contents

Introduction: How it all Started   1

I. Letting Go   9

   Change is Scary and Exciting   9

   Limitation or Expansion – There is a Way!   13

   Rigidity and Judgment Versus Freedom   16

   Release Resistance   19

   Shifting to Effortless Ease   23

II. Dealing with Emotional Baggage   27

   Dump It!   27

   Everyone has a Story – What's Yours?   35

   Challenge Your Story   38

   Victimhood: A Common Ego Trap   44

   Switch off Negative Mental Chatter; Switch on Self Affirmation   52

   Managing Conscious-Subconscious Dynamics   56

   Turn Failure into Triumph   59

   Be Bigger than the Problem   64

III. Develop Self-Expression — 67

    Take Responsibility for Your Life — 67

    Self-Expression – Find YOUR Way – Reduce Your Stress — 70

    Become an Expansive Thinker — 76

    If you need to do it – do it! — 79

IV. Be Your Natural Self — 83

    Authenticity and Naturalness — 83

    Panic Attacks – No Problem — 86

    The Purpose of Anxiety — 88

    Adjusting Your View — 90

    Relax and Get Real — 96

    You are Valuable – Acknowledge it! — 99

    Turning on Highest Intelligence — 109

V. Flow with Life — 113

    Motion and Change — 113

    Open to Possibilities — 117

    To Create Ease Forgive Yourself and Everyone Else — 122

    Live in Gratitude — 125

    Let go by Laughing More!! — 128

VI. Meditation: The Antithesis of Anxiety   **135**

   First: Move into Natural Rhythm   135

   Second: Reframe Your Mind – Make Love Your Center   139

   Third: Meditation as a Mental Discipline to Erase Anxiety   142

   Meditation to relax and connect with your Inner Guide   144

   Choices and Conclusion   146

Acknowledgments   **153**

About the Author   **155**

Introduction: How it all Started

Beginning the Journey

Smile, breathe, and go slowly.
Thich Nhat Hanh

Worry and anxiety are common maladies these days. People routinely have panic attacks and even live in fear of them. Yet there is a way around these problems, and it takes training. I'm not talking about knocking down pills, although people survive on anti-depressants and anti-anxiety medication for years, but there are consequences to that. A healthier approach would be to go to the root cause of the issue and make changes from there.

Anyone can do this. Making adjustments requires dedication, focus, and discipline. Yet anyone can do it. We have discipline to clear our schedule to watch a favorite sports team or go out with friends, and we muster up similar dedication to release anxiety and worry. What is more important than your mental health? Everyday stress takes a toll on your well-being and sense of joy and can even cut your life short.

In this book you will discover practices to help you move from anxiety and worry to peace of mind and you will read stories of people who have successfully made the transition. It is a process. Others have successfully transitioned in this way and you can too. It is like crossing a stream, jumping from rock to rock. Take a step and the next stone (step) will appear before you. The main thing is to start!!

My search for answers began with my mother. She was a wonderful mother, in that her attention was centered on her family and she did her very best. She was also incredibly resourceful and creative in her solutions. (There was the time she tore the fireplace out of the living room wall because she did not like it. She had her three children parading, hands full of bricks, out the front door and around to the backyard "ash pit" dumping their haul until the "ugly" fireplace disappeared from view.

At Prom time, cash was tight, so she cashed in our *US savings bonds* (remember those) so we could acquire the requisite fancy prom dresses.) My remembrance was that she always found a way.

She was the dedicated caretaker for her husband, three children and her own mother. She accomplished this with concern and love. Yet, during all of this, she had a major problem that taunted her. She was racked with anxiety, worry, and fretfulness. It made her existence tense and exhausting and took a toll on the rest of us as well.

Her constant and overwhelming fear expressed as a nervous condition wherein she could not sit still. She was always in motion, squirming, continuously busy… moving endlessly—sewing, paperwork, fussing, fussing, fussing. If you were in her proximity you could not avoid feeling her heightened emotion and restless energy. It seemed to fill the air and soon you were jiggling and jumping, feeling the same unease and inability to relax. If she were present today, she would be diagnosed and medicated, but that was then, and this is now.

My self-appointed task was to calm her, and I was as relentless in my mission as she was in hers (to continually worry). This often put us at odds.

My enthusiasm for my task was unending. Yet as a child, my efforts were limited by lack of experience and understanding. I would attempt to sway her perception as she dealt with a concern—always trying to introduce a different, more positive point of view. I coerced her to consider addressing problems with optimism. Example: Mom: *"Oh dear, the roof is leaking."* Me: *"It is good that you know about the leak because now you can get it fixed."* Yes, my attempts were simplistic, but they were heartfelt. I wanted her to have more peace. I realized later that my ulterior motive was to bring peace to my whole family, including myself. But working that out through my mother was not to be.

The issue was that her escalated anxiety translated into criticism and negativity toward everything and everyone. There was nothing right with anything. She had an expert's ability to find the flaw in every situation and person. She taught me well to do the same.

Bottom line, she was filled with fear and her attempt to feel safe evolved into trying to control everything, and, of course, it didn't work, as it never does. As a result, if you were the least bit sensitive (as I was) you started looking for flaws and anticipating criticism in everything you did in an (unsuccessful) attempt to avoid it. (Pay attention here because I am stating that on-going attention was laser focused on <u>what was wrong</u>? Note: what you focus on increases. Therefore, attempting to avoid negativity by focusing on what is wrong, yields to more negativity.) So, you can imagine how discomforting it was to live with such adverse focus. It led to an edgy, uncomfortable existence and I was determined to find a way out. It turns out that the problem I was trying to avoid (fear, anxiety, and criticism) became my primary focus and that never yields to positive results. Concentrating on what you don't want to try to arrive at what you do want is a navigational reversal. It is like driving to Texas to get to New York. Not practical as it doesn't work!

Since all efforts to change other people to make our own lives better is misplaced energy, after attempting various strategies to *get* her to relax, I gave up the struggle and decided that since I couldn't change her, I would find my own way to peace. In other words, I had to mentally and emotionally disengage from my mother's unhealthy condition as I was powerless to change her and I yearned for peace. That was a beginning albeit powerful step to freeing myself to find my own path to peace.

My determination led me to study. I knew there had to be a better way and I was bound and determined to find it. I dove into metaphysics, Universal law, brain pathways, psychology, Buddhism, Hinduism, the Bible, A Course in Miracles, The Life and Teachings of the Masters of the Far East, etcetera, etcetera. Wisdom opened to a compassionate heart. Yes, I discovered compassion and empathy for my mother who really was not healthy. (She literally and ultimately wore herself out with fear, nervousness and anxiety.)

Yet through my study and practice, I found peace for myself. Perhaps you have been involved in futile attempts to help someone who was not ready or open for change. If so, you will appreciate the effort.

Some of the tenets from my journey to peace are written in this book and if you practice them you will discover ways that work for you. Some of the practices are age-old and all of them are effective.

As you take this journey, you will realize that the mind is an amazingly creative instrument. We are only beginning to have an inkling of what is possible when we focus it properly. That is our work and our process. My hope is that these ideas trigger your own search. Yes, there is a better way, and yes, you can achieve a life free from anxiety and centered in peace.

Centeredness in the midst of chaos, in the resolution of a problem, and finding your way in the darkness of despair involves self-study and awareness. As Socrates declared, *know thyself*. That means to recognize and own our issues in order to rise above them. There are many shifts to be made and they are all doable. With growing awareness, the ever-present joy of Spirit expands within you.

The effort is worthy as it brings understanding of wholeness and deepest connection, perhaps even self-mastery. As we shall discover, the view from the top of the mountain is profoundly more inspirational than that from the abyss of despair. The higher you lift yourself with these practices, the more power and clarity you will experience. Would you rather be a spiritual giant (ten feet tall) or tiny, helpless and trapped in fear?

It is darn near impossible to feel secure and confident if you believe you are alone and struggling to get through life with meager resources. Yet other possibilities exist. By broadening your view, you realize that there are abundant resources and infinite possibilities—all for you to tap. With practice you will feel the freedom of your expansive nature. That is what these steps are about. As you take action, you will reclaim your innate power and freedom.

This study explores various methods. But first you must condition your mind to be open and willing to release your attachment to old ways, and insistent on seeking from a higher perspective and viewpoint.

Einstein said it well, *you cannot solve a problem from the same mind that created the problem."* Thus, with his guidance we seek a new mind and a new perspective. In the offing let it be known that it is fun to explore and change and it is glorious to find that you have the energy and insight to alter your vision and adjust your beliefs to embrace the amazing self you were designed to be. In fact, it is freedom.

There is a story that further explains this concept of observing life from a new angle. It involves a horse that was tethered outside a shop on a narrow street in a Chinese village. The horse was not happy being tethered and he made that plain because when someone attempted to walk past, he would try to kick him. After a while a crowd of people gathered and started debating how best to get by the angry horse. Soon, someone came running announcing, *"The Old Master is coming! He'll know what to do!"*

The crowd waited with great anticipation. As the Old Master turned into the street, he caught sight of the horse, and immediately spun around to walk down a different street. The Old Master knew the lesson of flow and accepted the situation as it was. He did not attempt to change the horse or the situation. He merely adjusted his movement.

That is exactly what I did when I ceased trying to "fix" my mom and decided instead to fix myself. That is what you can do too!

This book is set up in six sections. Each section explores an aspect of releasing anxiety and stress while training your mind to new potentials. There are exercises at the end of each chapter to instruct you in new ways to deal with challenges. The last section of the book concerns the practice of meditation. India's holy book, the Bhagavad Gita states that *when meditation is mastered, the mind is unwavering like the flame of a lamp in a windless place.*

It makes sense that people who meditate regularly are calmer, have more clarity, and demonstrate more stability. Meditation makes you happier. It establishes a strong mind that can overcome difficulties—all difficulties—and achieve dreams.

In the Meditation Chapter, you will be guided to the purpose of meditation and why it is an important practice to heal stress and anxiety. In these pages you will learn how to manage the mind and *still it* on command. You will also be given a guided meditation to train in stillness.

As you practice with the information and exercises presented in each chapter you will discover a heightened ability to bring the mind to task. By managing your thoughts, you will have created the mental discipline that allows a continuous connection to peace.

I. Letting Go

You don't have to control your thoughts.
You just have to stop letting them control you.
Dan Millman

Change is Scary and Exciting

This book is about change. Because you are reading it, there is a part of you that is ready to move from the mind set of fear and anxiety to the consciousness of peace.

Many people are afraid of change and this usually means they are afraid of the unknown. This cycles back to not trusting themselves. Yet, we may as well make peace with change because it is the only constant in life. Change happens... daily!

To change means to alter, convert, or transform the form or content of something. Change can be simple as ten dimes for a dollar or as complex as birth, death, marriage or divorce. But since change is the only constant in life, we can count on it and that is a good reason to align with it and use it to your own best good.

Change: day moves to night and back again. Spring flows to summer and fall to winter. Every molecule of your body is continuously changing. Life flows; your breath rotates in and out; food is digested, assimilated and eliminated. You sleep and wake in cycle. Everything is in a cycle of change—you are too!

In life we have choices every day and about everything. We can choose where and what we want to eat or how fast to drive, whether to be on time or late. The day is filled with choices. Growth is a choice. How we change is a choice.

Essentially, we have two choices where change is concerned—adapt to the process or resist it. In other words, you can joyfully greet change, or you are dragged kicking and screaming to new phases of life. Since change is inevitable, and the only constant, it is wise to embrace it with enthusiasm. Study it and let it tell you where and how you are to change.

For instance, you can choose to grow in health which might indicate altering your routine, including daily exercise, giving up carbs, or thinking more positively (to name a few possibilities), or you can physically deteriorate (avoid life, sit on the couch, drink beer, and cuss at the television, to name some possibilities). You can profit from the opportunities change presents and choose progress over stagnation and decline. Even though many people find change perilous and scary, it is the thing that makes life exciting and provokes evolution.

That is what I want for you. To face down fear and evolve in wonderful ways that fit your psyche and convert your life to fun and adventure. I offer the information and exercises in this book to help you do that. In my work with thousands of people, I can tell you they work.

Entertainer and sausage entrepreneur, Jimmy Dean, notes, *I can't change the direction of the wind, but I can adjust my sails to always reach my destination.*

President, John F Kennedy, confirmed that *Change is the law of life and those who look only to the past or the present are certain to miss the future.*

One of the ways we prepare ourselves to move from anxiety to peace is to get comfortable with change. By doing that you release a lot of worry and fretting as your first step. To get in the habit of letting go, regularly step out of your routine. Monitor your day and you will find that you have many routines (habits) that you perform day after day, and they keep you in a kind of mental hypnosis. You get up the same way, follow your routine from brushing your teeth to drinking morning coffee, when you take your shower and what you eat for breakfast. These habits carry you through your day and you become lulled into a mesmerized coma.

Start your preparation to change by taking regular physical, mental, and spiritual breaks. Change your routine, get your coffee at the gas station, take a new route to work, go in earlier or later. Consider a different job or call your mother on Thursday inside of Sunday. Try new foods, wear different clothes, talk to a stranger, you get it. You never wear pink. Good! Buy and wear a pink shirt. Change in as many ways as you can tolerate. And then change some more.

Soon you will want to choose a different item from the menu. You will look forward to the adventure of discovery. Facing and promoting change will help you develop *eagle* vision…. seeing from a broader perspective and developing adaptability.

Charles Darwin acknowledged that, *It is not the strongest of the species that survive nor the most intelligent but the one most responsive to change.*

Stay open to the possibilities by avoiding judgment, assumptions, and other ego traps. The ego is your small self and it wants to avoid growth and expansion. It does that by trying to control everything insuring the maintenance of status quo and smallness. When you think, *"My way is the only way: this how I have always done it. It is the right way and I am not open to change."* It is your ego talking and it is time to learn how to set it aside, so you can adapt to a larger, more interesting, and expansive life.

Lastly commit to learning from everyone and everything. Read, ask questions, and explore new experiences, places and people. Take classes, attempt new projects. Let go of perfectionism and go for the experience instead.

Life is filled with endless possibilities. Investigate as many as possible. The more information you acquire, the larger your range of choices, the more exciting your life and the greater your growth. What opportunities for expansion are present in your life right now? Which one would you like to begin investigating?

It is okay! You can recognize your fear of change and start with one small step. Change the flavor of your coffee. And then tomorrow, take a different route to work and after that you can plan a weekend adventure to a new part of town and just explore. Soon, you will have broken from the hypnosis of habit and begin to resonate to a higher, more vibrant frequency and you will feel more alive.

Jean Walters

Limitation or Expansion – There is a Way!

With realization of one's own potential and self-confidence in one's ability, one can build a better world.

Dalai Lama

My career as a personal and spiritual growth consultant, Akashic Record reader, and metaphysics teacher has spanned decades and I have been privileged to have touched the lives of thousands of students and clients. My work is inspirational as it involves lifting people (mentally and spiritually) to their highest potential. Since my youthful attempts to help my mother (my earliest training), I have chosen to shift my focus in ways that she was unable to do, by observing the blessings life offers. By living in appreciation, my energy stays high and my vision is broad. The fact is that when you look for gifts, you always find them.

As I ventured along my path, I developed a personal philosophy:

- that no matter the need, there is a way to fill it;
- there is no lack in the universe; and
- whatever you are seeking is also seeking you.

The Journey from Anxiety to Peace

The fact is that nature abhors a void and by consistently keeping your mind open, the vacuum of your need is filled. Someone comes along to guide or offer solutions or resources. You read an article or see something on television that triggers an insight, a friend shows up at just the right moment or makes an off-handed remark that prompts an ingenious idea. Life is ever one moment away from brilliance.

There is always a way. Our work is to be receptive as that is what it takes to let go of rigidity, willfulness, and small mindedness. Each person is a work in progress hanging out in an imperfect, temporal world while he comes to terms with his delusions of imperfection.

When we wholly identify with our physicality, we see limitation and lack. There are only 24 hours in a day and we must spend time sleeping and eating during part of that time. We may not be able to get everything done that we want. Yes, many things can be improved. Nonetheless by recognizing the magnificence of our indwelling Spirit, it is easy to perceive perfection. A tree is perfect, as is a bird and a flower. In your Spiritual nature, you are also perfect.

It is a choice and a discipline. From the moment you identified as a limited material being you accepted the karma of limitation. The secret (key) is to move your attention from the container of your vehicle (body) to the Spirit that occupies it. (When you buy a box of cereal, you don't focus on the box, but what is inside of the box, the cereal. That is what you must do with yourself.) When you shift your point of attention, the world as a mental construct immediately opens and new possibilities appear. Limitation or expansion—that is the ultimate choice.

Exercise – identify a situation that appears troublesome and ask yourself why you believe it to be so. I recently read a story about a woman who was deaf and believed she would like to hear again. Yet on reflection, she realized that deafness had served her in that she didn't have to hear the noise of anger, upset, or chaos. She didn't have to listen to the news and the railings of disgruntled people. She therefore understood that to give up deafness and engage fully in healing, she would have to agree to an intimacy with life she had avoided. She had to be willing to hear it all and give up the guard and protection that kept her isolated. It meant owning her condition and being willing to change and accept the process.

Each of us has envisioned and accepted limitations in our earth experience. To explore the depth of our inhibiting mental constructs so that we might make adjustments is a mighty commitment. If you were to deal with this pledge through the eyes of the ego, you might judge yourself stupid, wrong or inferior. However, by approaching this work as not only removing limiting mental constructs but replacing them with empowering expansive potentials that truly define who you are, you begin to see the power of self-actualization.

Worry and anxiety has kept you singular, separate and small. Advancing in this work of self-definition and healing will bring to full awareness a power you have yet to experience. By releasing all that doesn't serve you, you will discover a new task of self-discovery that is worthy of your highest commitment.

The Journey from Anxiety to Peace

Rigidity and Judgment Versus Freedom

Confidence comes not from always being right but from not fearing to be wrong.

Peter T Mcintyre

The idea of struggle has been built in (programmed) into the psyche of every person—*You must work hard to get ahead; struggle is part of life; you must push through; nothing worthwhile is easy; what are people going to think/say; etcetera.* These ideas are cultural propensities and there is a certain validity to them, yet there is another way to manage life and struggle does not have to be the recurring theme.

In other words, if you seek a better way, you will find it. You can become immune (non-reactive) to the push and pull and ups and downs of life and be centered and prepared for anything coming your way. Flexibility and responsiveness are achieved as you evolve your awareness and prepare your mind for new ways. Or to say it another way, per Helen Keller, *life is either an exciting adventure or nothing at all.*

Often people choose a life of comfort. That means they want a nice, steady, stable job where they can work until retirement. They want investments that expand readily and provide safety and freedom from worry, and they want friends and family to provide enjoyment but not hassle. In other words, they want a situation where there is no change.

Lots of luck with that because that is not how the Universe works. The Universe is about expansion, not sameness.

We are in the schoolroom of earth to grow and expand. Expansion means change—period! You can choose to embrace growth, or you can deny it, but the Universe is relentless, and in constant change and that includes YOU! Do you remember what it was like when you were an infant? How about when you were twelve years old? Do you remember your first love, or your first job, or graduating? With each experience a bit of you changes, grows, matures, learns something. Each step can add to your evolution if you choose to look at it from that point of view or you can stack up a lot of resentments and failures. Again, it is how you choose to process each event. The point is, you are not the person you were 20 years ago, or five or one.

When you push someone, his automatic response is to push back. This is called *resistance*. No one likes to be pushed. Yet, often people won't move unless they are pushed. Change is the push.

Along these lines, the tendency is to think that life should conform to our every wish and demand. Interestingly, I met two women both of whom had recently lost their marriage partners through death. And they were both MAD! One was incensed that her husband would dare to die and leave her alone. The other was livid because now she had to learn to do all the things that he did for her. Each felt that by dying her husband had broken a sacred agreement that they were to be married forever. Neither had contemplated that death was a possibility for either of them and neither had a clue that the opportunity at hand was to grow by facing their discomfort and learning a new way. It is called flowing with what is.

The Journey from Anxiety to Peace

Accepting the premise that life has to work the way you want it to, puts you at a decided disadvantage because there are always surprises and if you are not prepared life's twists and turns will be inconvenient if not downright annoying

A better way, one that offers less stress, can be cultivating a proclivity for natural flow and finding joy in growth. Learning how to flow with nature (life) and perceiving events from a higher perspective helps you accept change, get stronger, grow in confidence, and have more fun.

Behaving like a spoiled brat, stomping your feet, throwing tantrums and having pity parties when you don't get your way is anxiety provoking and leads to victim mentality, sadness and disillusionment. The problem is that Life (the Universe) doesn't give in to temper tantrums—other than to increase the pressure. In other words, negative reactions create more negative conditions and more negative reactions. It is the mirror effect (the world mirrors your inner feelings) and is unerring in its predictability.

Let's consider natural rhythm. The trees bud when the temperature and sunlight are just right. The flowers bloom in much the same way. The rivers flow according to rainfall and elevation. There is a pattern; it is logical and rhythmic. When we interfere with this natural pattern, we create chaos.

Just notice any country at war—there is grief, disorder, lack, and sadness. These conditions illustrate lack of harmony and natural rhythm. Someone wants to win over someone else…. a winner and a loser. Someone is right and someone else is wrong. Resistance, chaos, destruction, it can be external or internal and usually both. What is your conflict with yourself? Settle your inner conflict (resistance) and your world will reflect peace.

By the way, both women mentioned above found peace. They did this by accepting their situation of aloneness and agreeing to enter it and learn from it. It took a while, but appreciation for the years they spent with their husbands, and willingness to learn in their new situation resulted in peace.

Release Resistance

What you resist controls you.
Jack Schwarz, Healer

Recognizing the natural flow of energy goes a long way to experiencing a life of peace, joy and fulfillment. You can start by noticing the rhythm of nature, how effortlessly Winter yields to warm temperatures and flowers and trees burst forth in a vast array of color, shapes and textures. The climate warms yielding to Summer and outdoor activities abound. Fall follows gently, flowers cease their outward displays, trees erupt in glorious spectacles of oranges, reds, purples, and brown, and animals scurry to prepare for Winter, which brings stillness and retreat.

It is the same with man. There are cycles in life, and you can learn to recognize and accept them. Endings and beginnings. Death and rebirth. By choosing an attitude of peaceful acceptance, you release the need to fight, resist, and struggle.

The Journey from Anxiety to Peace

Listening to your inner rhythm will intensify and embolden your efforts and ultimately lead to the results you seek. That is the purpose of this book—to open the door to a life of rhythm, flow, and peace. Here is a story that exemplifies this principle of rhythm, flow and non-resistance.

There was a little critter that lived in the water near the bank of a river. It fed off elements within the river. Sometimes there was food to eat, and other times there wasn't. Either way, the critter spent its life clinging tightly to the bank because it was afraid. It believed that if it let go, it would surely perish in the sweep of the treacherous river's current. Its fear escalated when the current was particularly strong. There were days when the critter was exhausted with the effort of clinging, yet it would not let go because the prospect of being swept away to the unknown flow of the river was terrifying.

One day, overwhelmed with exhaustion, the critter could no longer hold to the bank. It finally released its grip and gave himself to the river. Tumbled and tossed by the tide, it was swept downstream and in a relatively short time, it landed in a beautiful pool of calm, pristine water. As the critter adjusted to the stillness of this newfound place, he looked around and saw that there was an abundance of food and it was obtainable without struggle. It dawned on the critter that if he had trusted the river all along, he could have enjoyed this peaceful, lavish existence sooner.

Thus, it is with each of us. We can let go and trust the river/flow (Spirit), allowing it to take us where it will. Or, we can hold on, fighting change, fearfully trying to control the status quo with struggle and effort. Letting go requires courage and faith. Holding on keeps you small, tense, and scared.

Of course, the river critter translates to you and me. At various times in our lives we have clung to the riverbank of our lives (the known) in fear of accepting the changes life brings and where it is trying to take us. Our greater good is to develop the strength, courage, and faith to let go and be moved to our next experience. It is to accept that something greater than our small egoic selves can devise a plan and by following Its process we can be led to an expanded experience that we may not ever have imagined.

The truth is that life (the Universe) is always moving us toward expansion and as we flow with it, we live exalted lives. That is the goal set forth in these pages… to offer the principles, and simple practices that will ultimately release you to your magnificent self and true freedom.

Letting go is a challenge and an opportunity. Some consider it weak, like fragility, failure or loss. Equate this to holding on to an investment while it loses value. You made the investment in good faith and, by God, you are going to hold on to it. This is misplaced judgment and short sighted. There are situations that start out fine and ultimately become toxic. We have all experienced them—jobs, relationships, even locations. Situations change, and you must adapt with them. The fact is that letting go is freedom. It releases you from the tired habits of the past and moves you to incredible new beginnings and personal expansion, just like the river critter.

It is said that what you resist persists (because that is where your attention and energy is focused). Resistance is struggle and what you resist has power over you. In other words, whatever you place your attention on, controls you. Healer, Jack Schwarz, stated the idea another way, *That which you identify with ultimately dominates you.* Therefore, if you fight fear, fear dominates you. If you identify with loneliness, loneliness controls you because that is where your attention is lodged. Resistance amounts to struggle.

There are many ways we fight life. By avoiding illness rather than maintaining health, we resist. Attention on debt rather than the continuous flow of money and opportunity is resistance. Assessing yourself as fat while you engage in dieting is misalignment of thought and amounts to resistance.

Abundance is a natural state. Look at any tree or bush and you will see millions of leaves effortlessly sprouting forth given the right conditions. A snowstorm presents millions of singular, unique snowflakes without any struggle. We resist life when we concentrate on all the ways something won't work instead finding ways it will, or by attempting to change other people instead of ourselves. Or by fighting evil instead of creating peace.

Life flows easily as does energy. There are only two ways to deal with energy. You either flow with it or resist it. Resisting wastes time and energy and creates struggle, stress, pain and negativity. Flowing opens the way to possibilities.

John was told that his job was ending, and he would soon be laid off. He started to object when he stopped. His inner voice told him to *stop, there is a better way just ahead.* So, John reached out and shook hands with his boss and walked out having no clue what this better way was but trusting his inner voice. Within a couple of days, John's friend Mark called and told him that he was starting a handyman business and he wanted John to be his partner. He said that John had all the skills that Mark lacked and together they would be able to create a great business. John immediately recognized that this was the *better way* his intuition spoke of and agreed to being Mark's partner. Together they built a prodigious business, and both enjoyed their newfound independence.

Nature is a great teacher of non-resistance or effortless ease. Instead of struggling against the wind, trees bend with it. Water trickles effortlessly down the mountain, flowing around obstacles, letting gravity guide the way. Animals know without trying, when to store food for the winter, build a nest, or fly south to a warmer climate. They do this with complete ease. We can live the same way. Listen to your inner rhythm and it will guide you to your next step, when to rest and when to be active, the answers you need, and the stillness you require.

Shifting to Effortless Ease

The struggle ends when gratitude begins.
Neal Donald Walsh

Effortless ease requires listening—to our bodies, our inner voice, what feels right. We block listening when we push forward relentlessly, without concern for stress and strain. Moving forward is fine. Do it in rhythm and flow.

Listening can be as simple as sleeping until you're ready to rise, eating when you are really hungry, working until you are tired, letting go of a goal that requires more from you than it gives, or releasing relationships that are toxic and unproductive. Each moment you give up struggle and resistance, you reduce anxiety and increase health, energy and personal resourcefulness. When you let go of everything that doesn't work or benefit you, you make room for everything that benefits. What do you need to let go of first!

Activity: Make a list of behaviors, beliefs, activities, habits and things you want to release. Prioritize them from one to ten (one being most important). Then begin with #1. Examine each item as to how you want to let it go. If it is a material item, you can give it away or throw it away. With tangible items the rule is does it give you pleasure and/or happy memories. If it is clothes, have I worn this in the last year and do I plan on wearing it in the next year. No!—Out it goes. Sometimes we hold on to perfectly good clothes that we will never wear again because our style has changed, or it doesn't fit. Guess what, someone else can wear these clothes and you will feel good to have given them up. By holding on to things that have outlived their usefulness, you are blocking energy, and that shows up in negative attitudes and reduced health. Too much stuff is distracting, stressful, and confusing.

If it is a habit or behavior, decide what you want to do instead. In other words, you can't give up something; you have to start doing something else instead. For instance, if you want to give up smoking, you might start being healthy instead. (What does that entail?) Don't get crazy here. Start with one or two items and that's all. Example: walking more, eating healthy, rest are possibilities.

With each release, be joyful. You are transcending to a higher version of yourself. You can make it simple by clearing out a drawer or closet. What needs to go; what have you not used or never will use; what can you let someone else have? You can let go of negativity by choosing to see the bright side of every situation. Let go! Let go! Let go! Focus on simplicity, order and ease as you go through your list. Let this exercise be fun!

As you make each change, feel the weight coming off your shoulders and your future glowing more brightly.

II. Dealing with Emotional Baggage

Nothing is worth poisoning yourself into stress, anxiety, and fear. He who is not everyday conquering some fear has not learned the secret of life. You have dug your soul out of the dark, you have fought to be here; do not go back to what buried you.

Anonymous

Dump It!

This includes memories of being hurt, offended, or criticized. Let it go! So, your mother didn't love you enough and your father wasn't there. That is on them and not you. Forgive them and move on. While you're at it, forgive your brother, your sister, your mean-spirited boss, your soccer coach, your nosy neighbors, and the rude store clerk. Let them all go. How? First, remember that what others project out into the world is what is inside of them. If you are an angry person, you look at the world through angry eyes and nothing is ever okay, and you are offended easily. By the same token, if you are kind, you see the world through kind eyes and are entranced. If you are looking for something wrong, you will certainly find it and if you are seeking beauty, you will easily find that as well.

Through their actions and words, each person is telling you who they are and that has nothing to do with you. Maya Angelou said it best: *When someone tells you who they are, believe them.* People are always telling you who they are through their words, actions, behaviors, and beliefs. It is great information to file away for future use. File it; don't be beguiled by it. This will save you trouble. If you want support, go to a supportive person and not a victim.

If you have made a practice of taking things personally, it is time to stop. Mostly this comes down to giving others too much credit and yourself too little. It would be lovely if everyone was kind and welcoming but that is not the world we live in. When we expect people to be more than what they have shown us, we are setting ourselves up for disappointment and pain. Become an observer of life and do it with detachment. Observe what others are saying with their words and actions. Their actions particularly speak volumes about who they choose to be. Your ability to discern *what is* in front of your eyes grows stronger each day when you choose to observe without attachment.

Expectations are mental constructs that get in the way of flow and they easily lead to disappointment and sadness. They keep your energy low because they keep your attention focused on the outer world.

Your inner world is full of promise. When you center your attention on your own capabilities, miracles can happen.

The truth is that anything is possible, and most things are available. Keeping your attention focused on your progress eliminates

As Sarah grew in self-awareness, she realized that her parents were the wounded ones and their dysfunction showed itself in alcoholism and the pursuant negative behaviors. Once she could see the source of her problem (wound) more clearly, she was able to let go of her self-defeating beliefs and move on in ways she could not before accomplish. Essentially, she changed the story she had been telling herself.

It all boils down to the fact that we are in charge of our own self-worth and identity and we cannot let anyone decide for us who we are. If you put your self-assurance up for grabs, you have lost control of your life and your future. Responsibility lies with you to heal your emotional wounds. No one can do it for you, and you cannot do it for anyone else.

Expecting the sun to rise each morning is scientifically valid. To expect people to act in a way that is inconsistent with their beliefs and self-esteem does not make sense and is delusional. Being disappointed when an angry person becomes angry is irrational and dis-honest. Angry people are going to be angry and happy people are going to be happy. End of story.

There was a young martial-arts student who was receiving instruction from a famous master. One day, the master observed a practice session and realized the presence of other students seemed to interfere with his student's attempt to perfect his moves. The master sensed the young man's frustration. He approached the student, tapped him on the shoulder and asked, *what is the problem?*

The student obviously stressed, answered, *I don't know. I keep trying, but I am unable to execute the moves correctly.*

The wise teacher said to him, *before you can master technique, you must understand harmony.* He took the student some distance away from the dojo and walked into a wooded area where they found a stream. They stood quietly on the bank for a few minutes when the master spoke. *Look at the stream. You see the rocks intruding on its course? Does it smash into them out of frustration? No, the stream merely flows over and around the rocks and moves on. To be in harmony, you must be like the water and then you will know what harmony is.*

The young man listened thoughtfully and took the master's advice to heart. Soon he was concentrated on his martial arts practice and barely noticing the other students around him. Nothing could get in the way of his focus. And he executed the most perfect moves.

Harmony with self is a skill to be cultivated. We are ever in process and each step in the process is to be glorified.

Action: Observe your thoughts for ten minutes. Set aside ten minutes—morning and evening and observe your thoughts. Take notes. When you have a *blaming thought,* stop and correct yourself. *Wait. I am responsible for my life.* If you find yourself feeling resentment or thinking, *poor me,* make an adjustment and alter your thoughts.

Sometimes you are tempted to ruminate, and it is exactly at those moments when you must catch yourself and interrupt your thought pattern. Deliberately change focus and think about something else: Bring up a pleasant memory. Remember a time when you confidently handled some situation in your life and you did it well. Keep re-directing yourself and eventually the victim thoughts lessen. By clearing out mental space held by grievances, you feel lighter and the payoff is huge… you are squashing struggle forever. You become harmony.

Always take time to create a new memory. When your mind focuses on what you really want, all the neurons begin to fire toward that new goal.

Soon, you discover ways to create the life you really desire. That is when life really becomes fun!

Everyone has a Story – What's Yours?

Identity is merely a pattern of events in time and space. Change the pattern and you have changed the person.

Nisargadatta Maharaj

One of the things that add tremendous stress to a person's life is the stories he tells himself and their impact. I knew a woman who was in her 70s and within an hour of meeting anyone she had informed them that her mother died when she was ten years old. Now it was true that her mother did die when she was young, but what purpose did it serve to educate random people as to that fact? What need is she fulfilling by telling that story?

Marilyn used this story to rationalize various development issues she had not deal with. She did not feel she had a role model for femininity (possibly television, movies, family friends might have provided a model). She believed she did not know how to be in an intimate relationship. (Actually, most people don't.) She felt awkward about relationships in general. Thus, the story, why am I not in a relationship—*my mother died when I was ten*. Why have I done this or not done that? *My mother died when I was ten*. And so it goes.

Almost everyone tells himself stories. I have heard lots of them. *I need to keep this job I hate because I can't make this much money anywhere else.* (Result: misery and stress.) *My parents taught me to be humble, never toot my own horn or say what I can bring to the table.* (Hence: no career advancement.) *I must stay in this abusive relationship because who else would want me.* (Result: low self-esteem and misery.)

These stories either increase or deflate energy. Your story expands or depletes your self-opinion and confidence. Stories can keep you hooked into anxiety provoking positions. Example: *I always get nervous around people; I am awkward, shy, introverted, backward, not good enough, not that smart, etc. I don't know how; I can't do it; I am a failure; I am Italian, Jewish, Albanian, European, a daughter of the American Revolution*—you name it. People use these labels to identify themselves and the labels conversely create limitation and with limitation comes stress. Each label carries a meaning, or it wouldn't be used at all. We provide the story to define who we are and then we are trapped by it. Can an orthodox Jew marry a Muslim? Probably not. Your story would not allow it. If you are shy and backward, can you be a leader or an innovator? Your story could pose a block.

When the woman who lost her mother at ten tells her story, she is explaining why she hasn't grown beyond the challenges of her early life. She was in a sense apologizing because she had convinced herself that she could not move beyond the stilted image she has created of herself. And, yet, in her life she had become strong and independent as she learned to navigate her path without the nurturing influence of a mother. She had been successful in a variety of ways. She built a

The Journey from Anxiety to Peace

someone down will make them bigger. Bottomline, it doesn't work. Never has, never will.

The trigger might be that *you did it wrong, you made a terrible mistake and that is horrible*. The truth is that is only one way to interpret a situation. By reducing the emotional component of that memory and thought system, you may realize that you made a decision that fit with a specific moment in time and your level of experience. Perhaps it did not produce the exact result you wanted and now you can re-do it *or* as your internal GPS objectively states, *"re-route."* In other words, don't overthink every reaction, it makes life HEAVY. Keep the emotional element minimized and, in time, you will eliminate the trigger all together. This helps you construct a new way to interpret events. One that is smooth, harmonious and peaceful.

Sarah grew up in an emotionally abusive environment. When her parents drank too much, they used derogatory language and called Sarah names—*stupid, a loser, incompetent*. As a child, Sarah looked up to her parents as children tend to do. They were her source of home and hearth. As a result, she accepted their alcoholic pronouncements, even though the truth was that she was a good student, did well in school, and her teachers thought of her as bright and creative. Her mom and dad, being key influencers and symbols in Sarah's life left strong emotional impressions on her young, vulnerable psyche and she felt shamed when she sought their love and approval and didn't get it. Her story-telling brain convinced her it must be her fault.

Her parents' cruelty left a gaping wound in Sarah's psyche. Thus, no matter her success in life, there was still a part of her that felt stupid and incompetent. Her ability to achieve her goals and live joyously were impeded by this wound and Sarah eventually sought psychological help to get to the bottom of her pain and lack of confidence.

32

Jean Walters

awkward in social situations but became known by his brilliance, his integrity, and his ability as a lawyer. He failed in a multitude of political elections for various government positions. Yet continued on undaunted taking the next step and the next step. At any point, he could have given up, but chose not to because there was something intrinsic moving him forward. He was a visionary and a great leader and ultimately became one of our most influential presidents.

In Lincoln's case, each loss seemed to build his internal fire. He had a part to play and chose to keep moving no matter what. And, he played his part. The question then is: What is your part? And, what resources are you developing as you move along? How are you preparing to play the part for which you were designed?

Memories (positive and negative) can help you recognize the lies you have told yourself. They can signal events that must be re-interpreted. To believe you are unworthy is an outrageous untruth. Can you imagine looking at a beautiful baby and thinking it doesn't deserve the best. Of course not! Yet, that is the position you place yourself by accepting the idea of unworthiness. In your true self you are as innocent as a baby and every bit as worthy.

By being aware of your emotional baggage and how you have distorted memories to make yourself feel bad, you will recognize your emotional triggers and know what needs correction. For instance, if you grew up in a family that puts people down and makes them feel wrong and humiliated, you have an opportunity to understand the source of one of your emotional triggers and STOP yourself from reacting when similar situations are presented.

The fact is that people who have low-self-esteem put others down. They do this to make themselves feel better. The illusion is that pushing

31

business, won prizes in sports, and had an interesting life. She really doesn't need to keep telling this story. She has grown beyond it.

When you tell *your* story, it is important to note if it has become a prison, a safe haven, an excuse, or a jumping off place. Just because you were born an orphan and spent years in foster homes and orphanages (like Wayne Dyer) does not mean you are any less equipped to manage life than someone who grew up in a *father knows best* family, or a modern version of the Waltons.

Living within various cultural, ethnic, locational stories can squeeze you into following traditions and cultural patterns that are not right or at the least, a bad fit for who you want to be. If you confine yourself within the story, you may not have room (space) to explore new, creative possibilities. You might feel loyalty to a family, religion or culture that negates options that work for you. To be clear your loyalty needs to be to your own growth.

Consider the stories of your life. How do you feel about them? Do they serve you? Is it time to let go or look at them from another angle? with different eyes? Possibly resolve them—rewrite a story or create a new one?

Are there challenges and difficulties you have blamed on external conditions or other people when what you are really dealing with is just a story that needs revision? Have there been opportunities you lost because you were attached to a story that precluded taking advantage of them.

Observe your stories. You speak them all the time—to others and to yourself. It could be a poor me narrative that has been there a long time and has repeatedly gotten in the way of living a joy-filled life. *Oh, wouldn't' you just know that I would get a traffic ticket, house fire, released from a job, lost a friend, etc.* (Name the pain.) Victim narratives keep you small, miserable and anxiously waiting for the next shoe to drop.

When you catch yourself in *story-mode*, step back and ask yourself if this yarn you've been telling is making your life better or worse? Is it increasing or diminishing your happiness? Is it blaming someone else for your circumstances? If the answer is yes, the story is generating angst, self-doubt, and stress, and it needs to go.

You are the one that can change it, revise it, eliminate it, and move on. As you master each story, you will find it easier to live without that particular drama and judgment. You will be able to look beyond each narrative for greater potential and be willing to address it as a matter of growth. With each step, you become calmer and more peaceful. Managing your mind is the way you release anxiety and stress and cultivate inner peace.

Challenge Your Story

I found I was more confident when I stopped trying to be someone else's definition of beautiful and started being my own.

Remington Miller

Get ready, it is time to examine, reframe, revise, or reconstruct your story to model the person you choose to be. You have the power and the creativity. Let's get busy and put it into practice.

In this book, you have read about many people and what they did or did not do to squelch anxiety, fear, and struggle. Now it is time to tell your story. To what do you attribute your current state of consciousness? Confidence? Success or failure? What was your childhood like? Adolescence? Adulthood? How have you trained yourself to handle difficult situations? How would you like to change this? What would be the first step? Let's start with writing your story. Here are some cues...

Your Story

What was your childhood like? (describe the energy and primary relationships and what you learned during your formative years.) Use descriptive words.

Adolescence... describe the energy, primary relationships, and what you learned.

Adulthood… describe the energy, primary relationships, and what you learned.

What have you noticed in your story that helps you understand how you formed unrealistic demands (on yourself) or *"what-if"* thinking about the future?

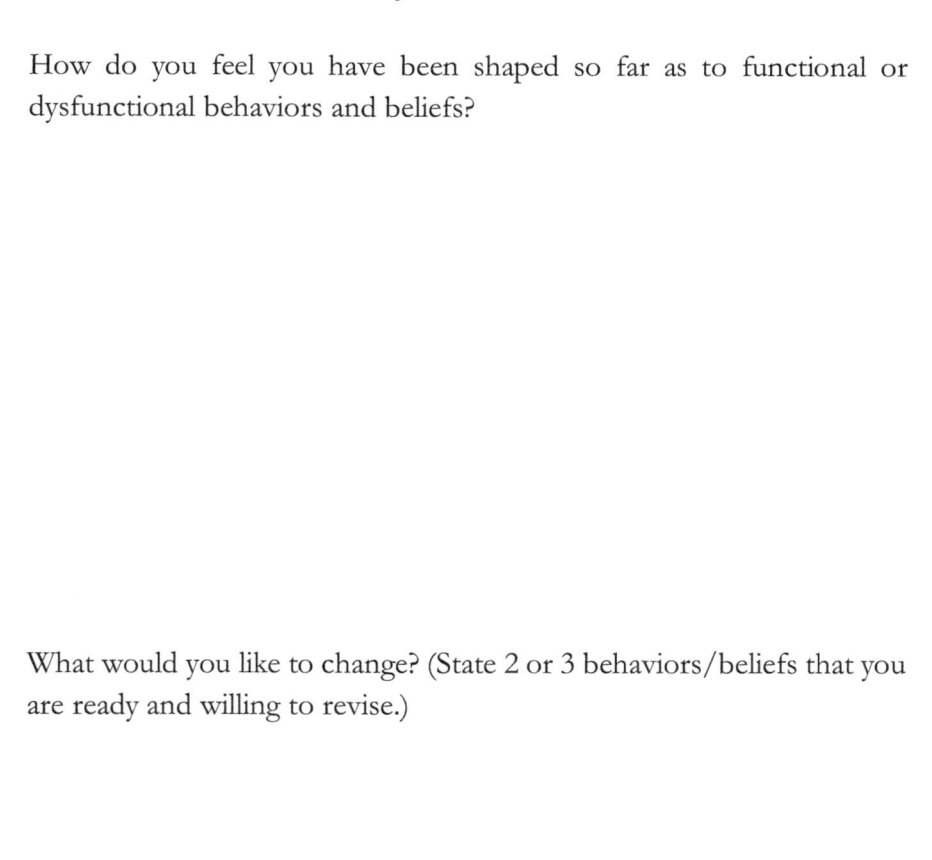

How do you feel you have been shaped so far as to functional or dysfunctional behaviors and beliefs?

What would you like to change? (State 2 or 3 behaviors/beliefs that you are ready and willing to revise.)

Pick a belief (Example: *Everything I do has to be perfect*) and challenge it. Why does everything have to be perfect? Is there such a thing as perfect? How can I replace this unrealistic requirement with something that makes sense? Example: *I am constantly learning and getting better and better every day. All my efforts are my best considering the time and circumstance.*

Belief and Challenge:

- About relationships:

- About health:

- About performance:

- About abundance:

- About wealth:

- About confidence:

- About career:

- About God / the Universe:

Perusing what you have read so far, what steps can you use right now to make some positive adjustments in beliefs or behaviors?

Steps to take now:

Start with the first step. Can or would you make a commitment to take the first step? This could be to get up ½ hour earlier each day to have quiet or reflective time or read positive literature. It could be to end a toxic relationship, take a class, join a new group of positive, focused, encouraging people. It could be to start exercising when you become anxious or make a commitment to bring yourself to the present moment when you are fretting about the future.

First step:
Victimhood: A Common Ego Trap

---

*Low self-esteem is like driving
through life with your hand-break on.*
Maxwell Maltz

Taking a victim stance is a common way people create anxiety and make life difficult. When you focus on mental concepts of limitation and helplessness, you are in victim consciousness. Victimhood, for the most part, has been taught. In other words, more than likely, you have come from a long line of folks who decreed victimhood. You know how it goes: *it is not my fault; he/she did it; I am not responsible. I always have bad luck.*

I have counseled hundreds (thousands) who decry their situation and place blame on the past—*my mother was cold; my 4th grade teacher told me I would never amount to anything. Someone challenged me: who are you to believe that you can be an artist, engineer, inventor, media personality, millionaire—you name it!*

The person attaching to these events has taken on a victim persona and allowed someone else's smallness, opinions, frustration, behavior, and/or negativity to shape his life. It is a gross misuse of influence, both on the part of the parent, teacher, friend, or supervisor, or whomever to decree such limiting statements **and** the individual receiving this instruction. Generally, people with low self-esteem let themselves be labeled this way, and, it becomes a great excuse for giving up their personal aspirations and dreams. As stated, a gross misuse!

I had a friend named Mel who told me that he was at a great disadvantage in life because his parents were uneducated and did not try to better themselves. He informed me that if he had different parents, he would have been much more successful.

This was his story, his fabrication, and he was sticking to it. What would have happened if he had decided that not having educated parents was going to be his motivation to become educated and to excel? We can choose how we look at any event. It can be optimistic and positive or an excuse to limit oneself.

Through all this, I was aware of a man who was born in an abandoned building and immediately given up for adoption. As a result, he was raised by a single mom on welfare. He had difficulty learning and was labeled *educable mentally retarded*. (Damaged goods.) The truth was that he had a learning disability and worked hard to learn.

Regardless, he had a dream to become a disc jockey and he would practice at night when he was supposed to be sleeping. Using his mom's hairbrush as a microphone he developed his patter and style and lived his dream in his room at night.

Eventually he showed up at a radio station and asked for a job. At the time, he didn't have nice clothes and was barefoot. He was refused a job and he showed up again and again every day until finally the station manager hired him as an errand boy—at no pay. But he did get paid because he listened and watched the DJs and taught himself their hand movements on the control panel and soaked up whatever he could until they asked him to go home.

Then one Saturday afternoon a miracle happened. The kid was at the station, as usual, and the DJ on hand had drank himself into unconsciousness and was unable to continue his program. The kid called the station manager who told him to call the other DJs and find someone to come in and take the original DJs place. The boy was screaming inside—*this was HIS moment* and he knew it. He waited 15 minutes and called the station manager to tell him that he couldn't find anyone to come in. The station manager then asked him, *young man, do you know how to work the controls? YES!* And with that he ran into the booth, flipped on the microphone and resolutely spoke into it, *Look out! This is me LB, triple P—Les Brown, Your Platter Playing Poppa. There were none before me and there will no none after me. Therefore, that makes me the one and only. Young and single and love to mingle. Certified, bona fide, indubitably qualified to bring you satisfaction, a whole lot of action. Look out, baby, I'm your Lo-o-ove man!* And with that the legendary Les Brown was born into his dream of being a DJ. And, that was only the beginning.

Hence, you see the difference between a person who is looking for excuses to not develop his talents and another who had every reason not to and does it anyway. It is all about choice.

Struggle is okay. It can make you strong and resilient. Life is not designed to hand you everything on a silver platter. Sometimes the advantage is in inventiveness, preparedness, working hard and jumping on opportunities.

You were born from greatness (Spirit) and you will go back to greatness when you leave this small material world. In the meantime, you get to choose the people and energy you allow in your life. Choosing is your great power. You can choose to be inspired (affected) by the beauty of a gorgeous sunrise or the giggle of a child or the complaints and putdowns of a person of limited vision. It is a choice.

Being a victim is a choice that is anxiety provoking. If you accept that role, life will always be a struggle because you are ever behind the eight ball. In other's words, the ideas and opinions of others mean nothing unless you agree with them. Hence, living as a victim becomes a self-sabotaging issue and yours to deal with. Addressing it requires new vision, reprogramming and repetition until it takes and holds. The truth is that there is more anxiety in keeping yourself bogged down in victimhood than there is in having a dream and working toward it.

As far as painful events go, everyone has experienced them. Some people wallow in the pain and rejection of the past, making anxiety a way of life and others rise up, leaving all that behind, while they move on to a new reality.

There is a story about twins who were put in two separate yet identical rooms, both filled with horseshit. The first twin sits in the corner and whines, *why is this happening to me. This is horrible. I don't want to be here.* The second twin starts shoveling because he knows that surely with all this horseshit there has to be a pony in here someplace, and, by gosh, he is going to find it. Thus, the first twin was stymied and overtaken with grief, fear, and anxiety and the second twin was inspired by the circumstances.

The point is, how you approach life and circumstances defines who you are and determines your influence in the world and with whom you interact. And, you can change this whenever you want to. Anytime you look out there (the external world) and let it control you—your mood, beliefs, and thinking—you have become your own problem.

The helplessness of victimhood is constantly worrisome and stressful. It stems from *other-orientation*. The solution is *self-orientation*. Those who are obsessed with what others think of them and how they appear in the world live their lives in fear. (Anxiety is fear.)

They try to manage opinions rather than themselves. Whereas, those who recognize Selfhood (they see themselves as independent, authentic, in charge of their life, and self-motivating), focus on what they want to be and do, just like Les Brown.

What can I learn from this situation; how can I improve my understanding and actions? are questions a self-reliant person considers. Self-orientation involves training your mind to hold the highest vision of your capabilities and possibilities. *What is possible; how can I go for it? What is my next step?* By focusing in this way, you release negative anxiety and life becomes an adventure.

I know a young man, *James,* who always wanted to work as a videographer. He went to great lengths to travel abroad to various countries to film the culture and people and tell their stories. He then edited and produced documentaries and informational pieces. He went so far as to live in South America for a year to integrate into the culture and get the right film footage. Yet, whenever he would get excited and motivated about his dream, his small self (ego) would step in with negative chatter. *What makes you think you can be a videographer? You don't have any talent. Anyone can do what you are doing? Blah, blah, blah!!*

All his excitement drained away because James let this disempowering head chatter tell him how it was. As you can imagine, James had to take control and decide what his priorities are and map out some action steps. And, he had to be consistent and ready to discount his old mental program of *not enough, not enough, never enough!!*

James' question to himself: *Do I want to live in defeat or move ahead and learn the art of cinematography? Am I willing to try even if it ends in failure? Am I willing to believe that I can do this?* In other words, is he willing to keep taking steps to develop his skills until he was producing the kind of work he could be proud of?

James had another common issue in that he was never satisfied and whatever he did was not enough. So, I made a deal with him. He would work on his film for a designated time (4 hours a day perhaps) and then take a break. The reason for this was when he worked too long, he got mentally tired and that is when he became vulnerable to the ego's negativity. In other words, he would start doubting his work. Working for a few hours and taking a break was a great way to use his talents at top energy and creativity and before fatigue set in. It worked for James. Perhaps it will work for you too.

We also made another agreement that he would do this work for me and not for himself. The reason for this agreement was that he had a history of not keeping his commitments to himself, but I was pretty sure he kept his commitments to his friends and I was willing to hold him accountable to his agreements. In other words, James did not want me to be disappointed. Therefore, he would follow through. (I don't think this is unusual. People with anxiety often have defeatist attitudes.)

These are the strategies we used to start a pattern of growth for James to become a cinematographer. Fulfilling any dream means taking steps. Just start the process. Take a step and that one will lead to the next one and soon you will have your magical moment and you have arrived.

There is a story in ancient scriptures that speaks of pulling up weeds in a patch of ground and leaving the ground barren. In time, the weeds return to that section of land and they are even stronger than before.

The Journey from Anxiety to Peace

The moral is that if you are removing negativity from your thinking, be sure to grow something new in its stead. For instance, plant and nurture positive, can-do attitudes and keep the weeds of anxiety provoking negativity crowded out. It is work and discipline and it pays off.

James' new self-statements: *I am a cinematographer. I have been assigned that task by the universe. It would not have given that to me if I did not have the talent. I am grateful to have been directed to videotape the world and I am willing to learn my way into the business.*

What is your new self-statement? Write it below. First get clear on your vision and statement and then decide on some action steps to move you in that direction. The clearer you are, the easier the journey will be, and the less you will consider each challenge to be a struggle. Plus, you will have more fun along the way. And, yes, fun is important!

Vision Statement (how you want your life to be). State it in present tense.

This is how I choose my life to be:

Action steps to begin the journey:

1.

2.

3.

Switch off Negative Mental Chatter; Switch on Self Affirmation

---

Each time we face our fear, we gain strength, courage, and confidence in the doing.
Theodore Roosevelt

It is important to not randomly accept other people's beliefs and opinions. People are most generous in readily projecting their beliefs onto others. It is called *transference* and it is important that you be picky about what energy and ideas you accept from others. For instance, if someone suggests that you are not making the best use of your talents, then more than likely, that person is not making the best use of his. If someone believes that nothing works out, then it doesn't (for him). That does not mean anything about you. If you are not aware of transference, you are wide open to being manipulated by others' negative programs. By being aware of transference, you can be steadfast in refusing ideas that are disempowering. Discrimination is important to keeping your mental field where you want it to be, in High Energy. Don't let anyone talk you out of this.

Then there is the idea of *"shoulding."* If someone lives with a lot of *"should* messages," it doesn't mean that you have to. *You should play it safe, You should do as you are told. You should never make waves or take risks. Blah, blah, blah.*

overthinking and obsessing about other people's motives because they are as much puzzlement to them as to you. In other words, most people are so disconnected from themselves that they don't know why they do what they do or feel what they feel. Ask them and they will confirm this.

If you are stuck on things that happened in the past, be aware that most people tend to remember emotional experiences, particularly if they are negative. The reason is they trigger your beliefs about yourself. Therefore, reinterpreting past experiences by recognizing they provided important learning opportunities, can be the key to change your valuation of yourself.

My story, when my twin sister, Jane, and I were in third grade, my mother, my teacher, Jane and I had a meeting. In this meeting the teacher stated that I was ahead of the class and could easily skip the next grade (they did that then), but Jane was on track with the class and would not be able to skip the next grade. She therefore suggested that I stay with the class because to do otherwise would embarrass Jane.

This experience affirmed to me that ***I was to wait for people***. That I was to forego my rhythm (which tended to be learn it; do it), and SLOW DOWN to honor the pace of other people. It also taught me that being smart was not as important as being normal. In effect, the underdog wins.

Yes, these were my interpretations and many years later I realized that I had been "waiting" my whole life for others to catch up and I decided NO MORE. It was up to me to reward my own abilities and move at my own pace. I have to tell you—the realization felt like freedom, like a weight came off my back. This is what I mean by reinterpret your experiences and find the good in them.

The Journey from Anxiety to Peace

Recently I coached a young lady who spent a month in Peru as a study-abroad program. She was fluent in Spanish, so it was easy for her to speak to the innkeeper where she and three other students stayed. She could interact with the teacher at the school where they were assisting, and she could interact with the children in class and settle disputes as they arose. The problem was that she thought the entire experience was awful. Why? Because none of the other girls could speak Spanish and thus she was always in the limelight. When I pointed out to her that her Peru experience pointed out her leadership abilities and there was no denying that she took control and demonstrated a propensity for knowing what to do in difficult situations, she began to see that there was another dimension to her study-abroad project that she had not considered. When she decided to take pride in her abilities rather than avoid them, her demeanor completely changed. This is what I mean by reinterpreting experiences.

Do you have moments that you consider *bad/negative*? Can you choose to see another possibility? Does failing math clarify that left-brain work is not going to be your forte and perhaps creative pursuits more perfectly match your disposition and talent? Does leaving a job that traumatized you need to be deemed a failure? What if leaving a toxic job situation is a sign of growth and maturity?

Life supplies many gifts and often we don't see them because we are busy judging with a narrow view. When we stand on the top of a mountain and look down, we develop vision. The question is: What was the blessing in this situation? If we ask the question, we receive the answer.

An abusive childhood may extend your resourcefulness or strengthen your resolve to become independent or innovative. Abraham Lincoln grew up in a log cabin and self-educated by the light of a candle. He was

There is no flow, excitement, or growth in *shoulding* yourself. In other words, figure out what works best for you and live by those principles. If you are wondering how to do that, the answer is to connect with your heart. (More on how to do that later.)

Along these lines, never let anyone put you down (and that includes yourself). If someone is coming from a place of negativity it may not be enough to recognize that he is talking about himself. You may need to let go completely. It is energy-depleting to deal with *Negative Nellies* and people who only want to see the worst in others. Many of these folks aren't satisfied until they are able to pull you into their world. By letting go, you create room for positive, optimistic folks to enter your life. But, this can't happen until you let go. Ah, a breath of fresh air! Letting go is freedom!

Recognizing these patterns helps you. It is like the Buddhist Monk who was told he was to deal with a negative situation. He said, *Good, I get to practice*. Yes, life is all about practice. In this case the practice is to decide what works for you. Letting others tell you what is true negates your responsibility to draw your own conclusions and will definitely lead to struggle, worry and anxiety—lots of it.

I had a client who bent over backwards trying to get her mother-in-law, *Dottie*, to *like her*. She cooked the foods her mother-in-law liked, and read the books she endorsed, and even changed her style of clothes to please her.

Then, one day I asked *Mary, what would happen if Dottie never approves of you? Exactly how would it impact your life?* Mary pondered this question and finally decided the answer was *nothing*. From then on Mary decided to do the things that she enjoyed—eat what she liked, wear the style that suited her, etcetera. AND, nothing did happen. If anything, Dottie was kind of impressed and she knew that she could no longer push Mary around. That amounted to growth for both of them.

You pay a heavy price for hanging out with *Debbie Downers*. It conditions you to expect the worst in every situation and makes you slightly crazy. If you get caught with a *downer,* take a break, go to a quiet place and let yourself download (release) the insanity and judgmental energy until you can get back to your center. Remember all the craziness of negativity amounts to a child throwing a temper tantrum. *I'm mad; I didn't get my way.* Let it go. Take a deep breath and blow it out. You are free!

Everyone has a right to a point of view. Even if you are wrong—so what! There is no need to debate, defend, or make excuses. As you understand your own position, you will grow stronger in your ability to state it confidently and then let go. If someone disagrees, so be it.

Along with weeding out negative people, consider releasing negative groups and thought systems. Don't listen to the news 24/7. Don't watch horror films and doomsday television. They carry negative energy and have a detrimental effect.

A person who smokes cigarettes cannot realistically think that his lungs are going to be healthy and a person who drinks heavily cannot believe that his liver is not burdened. The same is true with what you take in mentally and emotionally. Inundating yourself with violence, harshness, drama, and negativity does not bode well for your mind and soul.

Do be selective as to what and whom you listen to. Everyone exudes energy. Make sure you are around people who project positive, uplifting energy. In essence, connect with folks who are happy and have purpose. Hang with them. Of course, that means you will have to cultivate happiness and purpose. Yes, and doing this one thing will be a major factor in releasing anxiety.

The fact is that you are powerful and have the ability to change your life at any moment and in any way. You are powerful and each choice you make shapes your future and sets the tone of your life.

Now, moving to the heart. Not the physical organ but the inner space of heart intelligence. The heart is your highest intelligence. It knows beyond the intellect. Often people put all their efforts into attaining intellectual knowledge and believe their answer lies in what they understand from books and classes. These folks are often great at playing Trivial Pursuit games, but not particularly good at knowing what to do in life. They know what year every war started and ended. They know the square root of something and the chemical composition of something else. This can be termed intellectual brilliance and it is helpful when tearing down mechanical engines, building bridges and combining ingredients for a new medication. It is not particularly helpful for creative pursuits.

Heart intelligence reveals what is happening in your world and why. It guides you to the root of the problem and what it will take to solve it. It takes you to higher knowing and reveals the deepest meaning of an event or relationship and how to bring your consciousness to love. It goes beyond the surface of life and shows you the bigger picture and a greater outcome. It leads you to your deepest essence.

As you move from your head (thinking /analyzing) to your heart (feeling), you understand why people behave as they do and how you can deal with them appropriately. Soon you discover that in every negative situation is a lament about lack of supply, which amounts to lack of love. You also know if it is necessary for you to participate in any way. If the answer is NO and that means step out, let go.

Action: Do your own homework. Whether it's politics, news stories, or the best way to bake a cake, ask yourself what you believe about it before asking anyone else what they think. What makes sense to you? What do you think is the best way to balance the budget? Practice having an educated opinion and stating it without worrying what anyone else thinks. Own your beliefs and thought processes.

Secondly, practice going to your heart to check your decisions. Does it feel right? If not why? You can become extremely adept at listening and receiving answers from your highest intelligence. All it takes is practice.

Managing Conscious-Subconscious Dynamics

Love and peace of mind do protect us. They allow us to overcome the problems that life hands us. They teach us to survive... to live now.... to have the courage to confront each day.

Dr. Bernie Siegel

It would seem that every person has anxiety about something. Perhaps it is kids heading off to college, an unfulfilling job, divorce, looming retirement, or simply not having enough fun. All of these situations can lead to stress, but it doesn't have to be that way.

There is a way to face life head on, move through transitions, while actually enjoying them, becoming stronger and having more fun in the process. First let's take a dive into the mind and understand the dynamics of conscious and subconscious workings.

The mind is a creative tool and how we use it equates to the level of struggle we live with. For instance, if you are always *wanting* wealth, no matter how much money you acquire, there will never be enough. The reason for this is simple… the mental construct of *"wanting"* creates a belief of not having.

To really understand the dynamics of how this works, consider this example: You are playing golf and you tell yourself that *you are not athletically inclined, that your body is not conditioned for golf, that you probably will never be good at it, it is a really hard game, and there is no point in trying to get the little ball in the cup because it isn't going to happen for you.* You have just set up a powerful mental program and established it in the subconscious mind. This is just like downloading a program on your computer. In fact, it is exactly the same! Now every time you step out on the golf course your mental program clicks in and ensures that you will do poorly.

The subconscious mind receives this program and accepts it (in exactly the same way that a computer accepts a download). Consequently, it makes sure that you stand, move, and swing in such a manner that you do not get the ball to go into the cup. It does this obligingly and without question (like a computer). It might even help you pick out the wrong golf club and trainer to ensure that you fail at golf. It can make sure that you do not sleep well before a golf game, wear the wrong golf shoes, forget to hydrate, all to fulfill your program of failing at golf. The subconscious mind is your obedient servant. (Can you see the possibilities?)

OR, you might tell yourself that *golf is a cinch; a little practice and you've got this thing.* You play golf with gusto. You enjoy the scenery, the companionship, maybe even the competition. You KNOW that *you are a good athlete, golf is a simple game, and you are getting better at it every time you play.* By the same token, the subconscious mind unquestionably receives this program willingly and without resistance or hesitation and establishes the correct body movements, conditioning, and patterns so that you fulfill your chosen decree/program. It can even help you bump into just the right golf instructor or equipment. It is almost like magic.

Now, expand this concept of *conscious mind directing and subconscious fulfilling* to making friends, getting a job, creating wealth, being healthy, finding a solution, and having fun and you will see how easily people get themselves all balled up and completely stressed out and how others cruise through life as if angels are paving the way.

Here are examples of mental programming that creates stress: *Oh, the flu (cold, dysentery, or some illness) is coming around, so I will surely get it. My immune system is terrible; I catch everything. Everyone in my family has arthritis. I always get sick in the winter (summer/spring/whenever). I never get to take a vacation. Crap is always happening to me. No one likes me. It is hard to make friends, etc. etc.* You get the point. The fact is that the one thing we have control over in life is the mind and we exercise it by choosing productive, appropriate mental programs that allows us to live life to its fullest or to feel bummed out and unhappy. It is always a choice and YOU are the one making the choices.

Many people live in *"overwhelm"* because they are trying to please everyone, or they feel obliged to fix everything, or be everywhere, or do everything themselves even though help is at hand. This again, is the result of mental programming and the belief that stress is their lot in life and it somehow proves their worth. Bottomline—you are in charge. Take it! Sow the seeds of success, accomplishment, friendship, health and fun into your subconscious mind. Be diligent and speak positively and with passion every day. As you do this one day (one hour / one minute) at a time, your anxiety diminishes, and your peace deepens, and guess what, you are having more fun!

Turn Failure into Triumph

Think like a queen. A queen is not afraid to fail. Failure is another steppingstone to greatness.
Oprah Winfrey

It is important to pay attention to what you have previously called *failure* because this is where you can easily slip into struggle and anxiety. The loss of a job doesn't mean it's the end of the world. Instead it is an opportunity to find a better one or possibly start a business. It has been proven that most people will have many jobs before they complete their working career. As you pay attention, you will eventually recognize when life is nudging you to move on and you will do it with gusto. The question is: *Have I learned everything I need to from this job? Relationship? Situation? Am I complete with it? Is it time to move on? (Go to your heart for these answers.)*

The Journey from Anxiety to Peace

Often you will get signs when it is time to move along your path. There is more resistance to getting things done; you are not as motivated to do the job as you used to be; you are feeling a need to expand to other things; your inspiration lies elsewhere. Pay attention and take action as needed and your life will flow more easily.

Thomas J Watson, the founder of IBM, was not a stranger to failure. Watson ran afoul of the antitrust laws and was fired as the sales manager of the National Cash Register Company. At 40 years of age he was facing a jail sentence without home or job and with little money. Yet, even with this extraordinary pressure, Watson emerged to establish one of the most successful, innovative businesses in America. You could say that he learned by his mistakes and rose to success much like a Phoenix rising from the ashes. That is how failure works.

When a relationship ends, it may leave you feeling lost and disoriented. However, the end of a relationship may signal completion and indicate you have outgrown it, learned the lesson it was to teach you, or someone new is waiting to enter your life. At any rate, let go and move on. Instead of taking the traditional approach of blaming someone, choose to grow from the experience and you will have moved to triumph because you have maintained high energy and stayed open to new opportunities.

It is an error to believe that every job or relationship is to last forever and if it doesn't you have failed. The truth is that we regularly outgrow relationships and situations and when we do, they end. In fact, they must end because that is the only way you can go on to discover the people and situations that align with who you are now. Life is about expansion, not stagnation. Fighting to hold on to something that is in the throes of death is a losing proposition, whereas opening the door to new possibilities, keeps you young, alive, and inspired. Rebirth always follows death.

You are always in a growth process. That means you are not to stand still, but to keep moving forward. As you do this with optimism, and enthusiasm, you connect with exciting new people and possibilities. Change is growth.

Every relationship is for a reason, a season or forever. This means that there are lessons attached to each union. Some are to be understood and the relationship is complete, and other times people can learn the lessons together and create partnerships. Either way, life is about change and flow and relationships are a primary way we grow, expand, and learn. If you choose to see this process as evolutionary, you will find it to be exciting and fun.

By facing the unknown and turning *failure* into triumph, you discover more about yourself. Sometimes the gift is to understand that being alone and quiet can be restorative. You may need this. It can be the renewal you require to heal from the past and prepare for the future. Learning how to be alone prepares you to begin new friendships, impart on new adventures and build a fresh, new life.

Famed basketball player, Michael Jordan is an exemplary failure. As he states it, *I've missed more than 9000 shots in my career. I've lost almost 300 games. Twenty-six times I've been trusted to take the game winning shot and missed. I've failed over and over again in my life and that is why I have succeeded.*

And Jordan isn't alone in the *failure* category. Here are a few more examples of folks who failed in their initial efforts before they saw any glimmer of success.

Even though Bill Gates is one of the richest people on earth, he had his share of failures. An example would be his first business called, *Traf-O-*

Data, which crashed and burned when he attempted to present it to an investor.

Undaunted Gates and his partner Paul Allen moved on to form one of the most profitable companies in the history of the world—Microsoft. You might say that he learned a lot from his experience with Traf-O-Data and used these lessons well.

Former President Harry S Truman also failed in business. He and his partner Eddie Jacobson set up a hat shop in Kansas City. At the time, America was in economic decline and the business failed leaving Truman owing $20,000 to creditors. Illustrating his sense of integrity, he did not declare bankruptcy, but chose instead to pay back all the money he owed. It took more than 15 years. Truman's actions spoke loudly of his veracity and character.

Truman also knew defeat in other ways. He lost his judgeship in an election in Jackson County, Missouri. Undaunted, he ran again and was elected Presiding Judge. Through all his political dealings Truman developed a reputation as a man of integrity. No doubt, his response to defeat fed into that legacy. He wanted to be a public servant and because he consistently persevered despite failure, he rose to the highest position of service, the Presidency of the United States.

We are driving cars right now because of the genius of Henry Ford. His global vision was that consumerism is the key to peace. He acted on that idea by creating methods of mass production of inexpensive goods, high wages for workers, and systematically lowering costs. These principles resulted in technical and business innovations, including a franchise system for Ford dealerships. Yet, along the way, he experienced failures. His Detroit Automobile Company went out of business and the Edzel car bombed in the marketplace.

Everyone has the ability to turn failure into victory or success. As you study these remarkable stories, note the ones you identify with. Acknowledge the practices of those undaunted individuals and mimic their drive and determination. As you personalize these practices, you will find your own way to let go of disappointment and loss and move ahead. These people did not let failure get in their way. They viewed each experience as a stepping-stone to the next one and they got stronger, more resilient, more creative and savvier with each event.

A man with a beautiful, booming, resonant voice auditioned for a job as a radio announcer. When he was denied the job, he approached the decision maker and thanked him for rejecting him for the position because he knew that by not winning this job, he was going to find something better. And, he did!

Action: Do an assessment and write out your conclusions. First, look back at your life and notice what *failure* actually led to. What was the opportunity waiting? When did that unexpected turn in the road guide you to something better, more amazing and wonderful? You took a detour only to discover your soul mate. You didn't get into a certain school, only to discover a different educational opportunity that led to your dream career. These things happen all the time. What is your story?

Pause to ponder this: Is there anything in your life now that you consider terrible (not a fit)? And let me ask you this: Have you ever been wrong? Is it possible that this terrible situation is a path to a thrilling new escapade? If it has happened in the past, it most likely will happen again. And, if it didn't occur in the past, then it most assuredly will happen now—if you are open and willing.

Do a personal audit and you will be amazed at how what you thought was a failure was really just a directional change. You know, *re-routing*.

Consider another idea and as you look back to assess your life, were there some opportunities that you could have taken advantage of and didn't? What would have helped you recognize these potentials? Are you willing to explore new prospects today?

The bottom line is to look at each *supposed* failure and reinterpret it to recognize the possibilities that it opened for you. Are you willing to follow up on these potentials or are you fixated on the idea of failing? Pondering new potentials can help you relax knowing there is a lot available to you!

Be Bigger than the Problem

To establish true self esteem we must concentrate on our successes and forget about the failures and the negatives in our lives.
Denis Waitley

The human egoic mind loves to focus on what is wrong—the problem. And when it is given license to do that, the result is unhappiness. Centering on what doesn't work or what isn't magically fixed according to your personal timetable brings on frustration and anger. It is the trick of the ego to run our lives—to be in control of the mind, mood, and outlook and to consider the worst possibility. But it doesn't have to be that way. The truth is that who we are as energy, Spirit, and possibility is way bigger than the small ego centric, fear-based mind.

A New York resident hosted visitors from a small town to his city. It was the first time they had been to a big city and they were overwhelmed and thought the place awful, dirty, and chaotic. So, Tom, the New Yorker, decided to take his friends to the top of the Empire State building. He did this in the evening when the stars were bright, and the city lights were gleaming. In their view from the top of the building they could gaze out over the vast landscape and the sparkling city lights and observe the movement and flow of the people. From this vantage point, they were able to see the beauty and life flow of the city. *"It is like a dance!"* they exclaimed. *"It is beautiful!"*

Hence, we discover that the point of view you take makes the difference in how you judge a situation. As you move above specific circumstances and observe them from a higher dimension, possibilities open.

The ego loves to keep the mind clamped down in judgment and it will always find *the problem* and what is wrong. Yet, at any time, we can walk away from the doldrums and drama of earthly life. We can let go of anxiety and annoyance and shift our perspective and as we view circumstances from a different angle, we become aware of other choices and freedom.

Jesus repeatedly went to the mountain to pray and meditate. We must do the same. We lift ourselves to a higher perspective to release ***into*** our Greater Mind those things that seem bigger than we are and discover they are not. From this lofty perspective, as we revel in the lightness and freedom of Spirit, material concerns disappear. We once again acknowledge that I AM greater than this moment and situation. The secret or the art to maintaining this higher focus is to remember to be in the world but not of the world. And, as we do that, we can journey through life without getting hooked into drama, impatience and fear. We can experience joy!

The mind moves faster than the body and the world. We can see the correction and completion of the problem and yet it is not corrected or completed as fast as we want it to be. We are in a process. We must be willing to see it finalized and yet go through the motions, step by step. Slow down; enjoy the process. With each step our mental vision syncs closer to material reality and with each action you learn something new.

We must learn to go to the mountain (high place). In a way we must live there. We can view the earth as a movie or theatrical play from this high vantage point, but we never leave the mountain. The mountain is our home.

III. Develop Self-Expression

Take Responsibility for Your Life

*Confidence comes with maturity,
being more accepting of yourself.*
Nicole Scherzinger

Take responsibility for your life. All of it! When you let external conditions control your destiny, you surrender your power and authority to create the life you want. (Behind every material condition there is a spiritual cause that offers an opportunity for maturity and growth. By the same token, when you let someone else run your life (parent, boss, spouse, teacher, friend), you keep yourself stuck and without purpose. You become the victim and that makes you helpless and powerless.

Victimhood goes against Universal flow because you were not designed to be a victim. Victim status demands disavowing your innate drive and passion for self-expression. It keeps you trapped in smallness and fear.

The Journey from Anxiety to Peace

Your inner passion is the Universe speaking through you and it will not be denied. It is always present whispering to you, urging you onward. The truth is you may not be able to control all your circumstances, but you have total control on how you respond to them.

The drive to express can create anxiety if you don't yield to it. Sometimes nervousness indicates that there is something that needs expression. Holding back exacerbates anxiety. Speaking or acting according to what feels best in your heart alleviates stress and promotes a sense of freedom. This is because you have released trapped energy.

I knew a fellow who reacted with anger whenever something did not go his way. I asked him if he had a Plan B. In other words, if one way didn't pan out as expected, was he prepared to try something else? He looked at me askance. *"What?"* The concept of having various strategies at the ready was beyond him. Well, I could see that if all you had to move forward with was Plan A and your total investment was in that, it would certainly be disconcerting if it failed. That does not change the fact that we have to be prepared to pull ourselves up and brush ourselves off and try another approach. (Think of Bill Gates, Harry S Truman, Michael Jordan and numerous others.) It is smart to have Plan A, B, and C. Some people have gotten to Plan D, E, and F before the mountain moved. But it did finally move!!

There are many couples that found that having children biologically did not work out for them. If they did not pursue other means (artificial insemination, adoption, being foster parents) they would be childless. But they put their goal of having a family foremost and did not stop until they found their right way to make it happen. In other words, you can become a nervous wreck if things don't go as planned, or you can devise another strategy.

Everyone is creative, and creativity *must* be expressed. Build something. Write something. Learn to draw or speak, decorate a room, fix a motor, or program a computer. Everyone needs an outlet to express energy, one that is uniquely his own. Experiment until you discover yours. Your unique quality is your gift to the world.

One retired gentleman visits an elementary school weekly and reads to the children. He loves the kids. They love him, and the teacher loves that her students enthusiasm for reading has escalated.

Another retired fellow took school children on nature walks and instructed them on various plants, trees and animals. Everyone looked forward to the educational opportunity and getting out in nature. It gave the kids a break from the classroom and the gentleman a sense of fulfillment and purpose. And, of course, the teacher got a break too.

For many years, I taught a class called **Changing Career Direction: Finding Your Passion**. In this course the students explored their life-long yearnings and inner urges. As the class progressed, they became aware of what they loved to do and concocted ways to express their creativity as a hobby or career. By connecting with their unique creative impulses, students have gone on to develop a DJ business, various careers in writing including travel writing, cake decorating business, owning a bed and breakfast, opening a flower shop, lawn care business, and creating a concierge business. Each person lit up when he recognized his passion and felt vindicated to express it. Each found ways to implement it in his life. It was joyful! Everyone has a passion, and everyone can find a way to express it.

The interesting thing is that if you choose to withhold your innate passion, the tendency is to become nervous and anxious. The reason for this is that there is an energy that wants to come through you in urges, ideas, images, or music, and it demands an outlet. If you hold back, this energy builds up and eaks out in nervous energy. Everyone needs an outlet for creative energy and if you combine your love of doing something with creating an income, you have the best of both worlds. Giving your creativity to the world is called service.

A dentist uses his day off to entertain his love of photography. An IT specialist travels and takes exquisite photos which he develops and frames. A financial-expert paints canvasses in the evenings. These folks are balancing their left-brain daytime activity with right-brain creative activities. It is called balance.

An insurance agent coaches kids sports teams in his off hours. He loves coaching, he's good at it, and the kids love his help.

Doing what you love brings release, peace and fulfillment. It is important to explore your particular need for expression. Start it as a hobby and see where the energy takes you.

Action: Start with activities that come easy for you—decorating cakes, coaching a soccer team, organizing, making friends. Then expand on that. If you're not sure how to do that, take classes until you discover a way that feels right for you.

You don't have to be a Picasso to paint or a Hemingway to write. Teaching, volunteering, sales, fixing things, accounting, and business—these are all creative endeavors. In fact, anything can be done creatively. Don't worry about monetizing your efforts. Just do it for fun. In our world there is a tendency to nail every effort to money, but it is not necessary. Some things need to be done purely for love. And when you do them out of enjoyment you often find ways to offer these same talents as services for pay. Don't limit yourself.

By honoring yourself for the gifts you bring to the world, you drop the idea of comparing yourself to others and, at the same time, develop a deep appreciation for the diversity of skills that other people offer. Essentially, whatever you need is available. Someone has the exact talent that you require in any given situation.

Sharing your skills as a gift expands your influence in the world. Each skill and talent is placed perfectly with the person offering it. There is no confusion in the Universe. Just as a symphony orchestra is composed of many different instruments and musicians, each playing an important part in creating beautiful music, the Universe has its own symphony that depends on each individual's talent to complete the harmonic resonance of the world.

The orchestra requires every musician and the Universe needs you to play your part. Don't underestimate the ripples you have made in the pond of Universal energy and the people you have touched. When you examine each interaction and experience from a cosmic level, what you see is a miraculous synchronicity of flow and connection. All is good.

I have a friend who is a professional counselor. She asked me to sit in on one of her counseling sessions and offer critique. She had concern that she might be missing something and wanted feedback as to how she could improve her counseling skills. I agreed to meet with her and when the day came, I sat in on her session with a client as an observer. When she closed the session, she asked me for critique. I acknowledged that I thought the session went well. She had great connection with her client, and provided good feedback and things moved along well. I didn't have any negative criticism to offer because her session flowed naturally and proved helpful and productive. In fact, I thought she did a really great job. When I stated my thoughts, she became upset.

No, she said. *It can't be good. It is too easy.* Hence, we discover that there are many people who are gifted in their work and it comes easy for them. Often, when things seem to flow easily, we doubt it. As my friend noted, it is supposed to be harder than this so I must be doing something wrong. Not so! That is the confusion of the egoic mind. The truth is that when you are in your grove and expressing your natural abilities, things do flow smoothly and easily. Accept it!

I think of people as having a certain DNA that fits exactly with what they are doing. There are those who can listen to an engine and instantly know how to fix it and someone else can glance at a ledger and note exactly where the mistakes are. They have the exact right spiritual DNA for that particular work.

We have been brought up in a world where struggle is the norm. There is a popular saying, *No pain, no gain.* That is misleading. It has encouraged the belief that we must struggle to reach our goal or to be good at our craft. That is what my friend thought. If it came too easy, she must be doing something wrong. That is not the truth. In fact, struggle is often a sign that you are in the wrong business. If you are anxious at work, reassess. Are you doing the work that fits your natural abilities?

Contemplate what comes easy for you and construct a path to use those natural skills in considering work or career. If you approach work from that point of view, your anxiety will be radically reduced.

There are those who are naturally empathetic and make great counselors and others who are athletically superior and need to follow that path. Some folks are artistic, and others are good at breaking down concepts and teaching them to others. Some people are great storytellers and that talent can convert to writing, teaching, or acting.

I knew a woman who was gifted at anything involving computer technology. She told me that when she is problem solving computer issues, she would imagine herself inside the computer and she would *see* what needed to be fixed. Everyone has something.

Follow your natural instincts and see where they take you. I had a student who enjoyed visiting junkyards and sifting through junk. He would look for interesting metal pieces, which he took home and welded together. In the offing he converted junk metal into beautiful metal sculptures. He loved it. It was play for him. In time, he started a side business selling metal art.

There is a lot to be said for constructing your work around your passion and turning it into play. Successful people love what they do. Loving your work is a sign you are on the right path and it is a great way to release stress and access your "inner child." That is when your work becomes your play. You cannot be anxious if you are having fun.

Steven Spielberg, the great Hollywood producer and director, started shooting film when he was a child. He used his home as his studio and set up movie sets in various rooms. His friends were the actors and they would devise costumes and scripts. Each day they would act out and film a new drama.

I can imagine his mother dealing with her house being transformed on a daily basis and stepping over equipment and stage props as she went about her business. Is there any doubt why Spielberg got into the movie business? Of course, he went into film. It was the most natural thing in the world for him to do. In fact, it was the only thing to do. On the other hand, he would probably have been a wreck if he decided to become a computer geek, engineer, or scientist. Yuk! Not a fit!

Psychologist Mihaly Csikszentmihalyi has termed this sense of naturalness and rhythm *flow*. He thinks of it as being in a zone where the person is totally absorbed in what he is doing, completely involved in the activity for its own sake. Each thought and activity naturally proceed from the previous one. Your whole being is involved and you are using your abilities to the utmost. He uses playing jazz as an example of this kind of flow. It is interesting to note that jazz great, Louis Armstrong, stated the principle this way. *If you have to ask what jazz is, you'll never know.* That's flow. That is what we want to achieve because when we are in flow, there is no anxiety, no stress.

Become an Expansive Thinker

With realization of one's own potential and self-confidence in one's ability, one can built a better world.

Dalai Lama

This might sound counter-productive for a person with anxiety, but that isn't true. Expanding one's perspective reduces stress as it moves you into vast energy and vast potential. Anxiety, on the other hand, can lead you into obsession with minutia. Your tendency would be to try to control everything. It doesn't work and the result is more stress.

Becoming an expansive thinker can be as easy as standing on the edge of a large open field and gazing at the vastness of the field and the sky. (This also works with a mountaintop, an ocean, a forest, or a huge lake or any open area.) FEEL the spaciousness!

Train your mind to walk into any situation, meeting, or event and feel that same spaciousness. The idea is to *cultivate* the feeling of expansiveness. It is like reversing the idea of a small, helpless self and choosing instead to observe your situation as a vast consciousness (yours) gazing at a spacious world. As you nurture this feeling of expansiveness, you will experience greater command in every situation. You will also feel calmer because you are now living in vast, spiritual energy and that reflects who you truly are.

When you look at a person, relationship, or opportunity, ask yourself, *"What are the possibilities here?"* Most people don't see possibilities because they never ask the question. You must ask the question to *seek the* possibilities. What if joining a study group opens up opportunities to learn new skills, meet amazing people, or start a new career? What if taking a new route to work reveals a short cut, a new restaurant in town, or a beautiful view. Be curious and try new things. In fact, make newness and possibility an everyday event. Look for them. Make a date with yourself to do something new each week. It will expand your consciousness and keep you unstuck, free and expanding through newness. By pursuing this way of life, smallness, anxiety and worry diminish. You can think of it as a spiritual practice.

Action: Start by making a list of all the possible ways you can accomplish something. Pick a subject and write it down at the top of the sheet of paper. For instance: If you want to go back to school and you need tuition money, consider all the ways you could possibly receive it. Here are some ideas: You can take the money out of savings, get a school loan or grant, procure a home equity line of credit, ask someone to help you, create a *GoFundMe* account on the web, put it on your credit card, win the lottery, trade services with someone for paying your tuition, get a job that subsidizes schooling, join the military so it will pay for your college, win a contest, find a benefactor, and so forth. These are a few possibilities, but you can come up with more. If you are saying to yourself, *that won't work; that won't work,* etcetera, ignore that limited kind of thinking. It is restrictive and keeps you in struggle mode. Open your mind to possibilities—there are hundreds. As you cultivate this kind of vast possibility exploration, an idea will present itself and you will know that it will work, and you will be on your way.

I had a student who wanted to go back to college to get her Masters' degree but didn't think she could do it because she didn't have the money. (This is called narrow or limited thinking.) I suggested to her that inasmuch as she was a single mom with three children, she should check out the possibility of getting a grant at the University for single moms. She did indeed check it out and ended up going back to school and her masters' degree was paid for in full, with a grant. Voila! It doesn't have to be hard.

Remember James, the fellow who wanted to be a videographer? He entered a contest to make a video with specific criteria in a 48 period. His video drew attention from a TV station. From there he was invited to visit an actors' studio, a networking event for media folks, and was able to set up meetings to further his career and training. It all started when he opened his mind to possibilities.

The truth is: there is always a way. Start by writing out every idea and possibility and as you do this more will appear in your mind. Then start exploring some of these. You will find that as you make the phone call or meeting, you will discover that there are possibilities that you would have never thought of, but they do exist. Learning to explore in this way will change your life because you will begin to understand that there are NO limitations in the Universe.

Have you heard about the girl who lived at a homeless shelter and received a full college education on scholarship? Don't let your circumstances or limited thinking get in the way. There are always ways to accomplish anything. Taking yourself seriously and following up on your desires will bring calm to your thinking and your life.

If you need to do it – do it!

True beauty is the flame of self-confidence that shines form the inside out.
Barrie Davenport

Take-action and stand by it. Think Nike—just do it! That means leave a miserable job or relationship, relocate, take a class, try a new career—start over. Your life is your journey. If you are not growing, you are not going to be happy. Add to this the fact that the world is constantly changing, and you must too. Don't resist change because that is what causes anxiety and struggle. Embrace change. The only constant in life is change. So, learn to go with it. In fact, let change be your adventure.

The Journey from Anxiety to Peace

Years ago, I resisted becoming computer literate. Then one day I realized that even extracting money from a bank ATM machine required using a computer. So, yes, computers were the future and I didn't want to be left behind. And even though technology is not a natural fit for me, I have learned to make peace with it and use it to the best of my ability and it has, indeed, created many blessings and opportunities for me. I needed to do it and I did it.

The boxing great, Evan Holyfield offers a great example of someone who needed to take a stance, failed a few times, and persevered to achieve success. Holyfield developed tenacity when he was young. As a kid he fought another boy and lost. When he went home and told his mother, she didn't miss a beat and told him to *Go out there and fight him again*. So, he went out and battled the kid again and lost again. When he arrived home a second time, his mother repeated, *Go out there and fight that kid again*. So it turned out that Holyfield fought the other boy four times. The fourth time he won.

By that time, Holyfield had learned to stay cool and observe his opponent's weaknesses. Ultimately, he used his developed observation skills to recognize the weaknesses in all his opponents. As a result, Holyfield matured in his ability to use his opponents' weaknesses to his advantage. In that way he transformed what was initially a fear reaction into a studied response. The outcome was that Holyfield became a prize-winning boxer and champion. He needed to do it—and he did it!

Action: Make a list of things you need to do or want to change. Pick the first item and DO IT!! Do not factor into this list that you must be amazingly gifted with each item. Do it because it needs to be done. Do it for self-gratification, not applause.

Start with something small and work up to the bigger items. Maybe it's as simple as always hanging up your clothes at the end of the day or walking on a treadmill before you start your day. Perhaps it is time to release that extra 15 pounds you've been carrying around. Or, organizing your desk before you leave work. You could even get adventuresome and start a conversation with that good-looking guy at the coffee house.

If you want to develop a new skill, find a mentor or take a class. Learn something new. How about a class in computers, Zumba, finances, tap dancing, or a foreign language? Perhaps you'd like to investigate the travel industry, or how to start a bed and breakfast. Maybe you've always wanted to be an artist, so start with a beginning art class.

If you keep competition out of your learning experience, it can be pure fun. If you want to reduce stress and anxiety, sign up for a meditation class, yoga, or Pilates. There are many ways to stretch yourself (literally). The key is to not let yourself get comfortable. Comfort can be your enemy and it dissuades growth.

John Paul DeJoria was the son of first-generation American parents who immigrated to the US when he was just a baby. The family was poverty stricken and even as a child, DeJoria tried to help make ends meet by selling newspapers and Christmas cards. Despite their efforts, the family was not able to support themselves and as a result, John Paul was forced to enter the foster care system.

From there he got bounced, got involved with crime, joined the military, and worked as an employee for Redken Laboratories. At one point, DeJoria was living out of his car. It was then that an opportunity presented itself and he was able to get a $700 loan to create John Paul Mitchell Systems (hair products). DeJoria went to great lengths to sell his products, even going door-to-door. His determination yielded results as he ultimately built a brand that is worth many millions.

DeJoria didn't stop there as his undaunted spirit led him into the liquor industry as he created Patron tequila. Now, DeJoria is worth billions and he dabbles in many industries. From a child who struggled, he did what was necessary to build a name, a brand, and a fortune. He did what he needed to do to survive and from there he grew exponentially. You can too!

IV. Be Your Natural Self

Authenticity and Naturalness

Embracing your true self radiates a natural beauty that cannot be diluted or ignored. Confident, powerful, untamable, badass you.

Steve Maraboli

Albert Einstein said that you cannot solve a problem from the same mind that created the problem. Thus, the point in this chapter is to learn how to live beyond anxiety and struggle by assuming your natural flow and authenticity. That is the goal. It is accomplished one step at a time.

In this section I am offering universal principles that support the energy of flow and authenticity. These principles are simple to understand, and they require consistent practice to become part of your well-being. There is a reason for that. The reason is that you have been instructed to worry and fret all of your life. This has occurred through all sorts of means—school, friends, religious doctrine, literature, television, movies, history, and family. The idea of worrying about your family has even been exalted as a form of love. It is NOT! Worry is a mental construct that obstructs flow and naturalness.

The ego has been trained to ignore natural rhythm, at times even forcing nature to do its bidding—changing the natural course of a river; building flood walls; the atomic bomb; water, earth, and air pollution; drilling and fracking for oil that puts thousands of miles of landscape in jeopardy. Other ego constructs: our inability to properly rid nuclear waste or convert to clean energy; investigative reporting that has been reduced to sensationalism; corporate decisions that place profits ahead of people's welfare therefore putting thousands at risk for toxic poisoning; and medicine that poisons the body.

These are a few examples of global toxicity. Along the same lines, you will find the ego (false self/ personality) pushing and forcing you out of natural rhythm in your everyday life. Examples: overflowing schedules, rushing, perfectionism, impossible deadlines and quotas. There are people who would do anything for money—harm others, steal, and lie. They believe they are making progress and getting ahead, yet actually they accrue mighty karmic debts which come due at some point.

We have access to marvelous inventions: technology makes the events on the other side of the world instantly known (people can be assisted when a tsunami strikes, or an earthquake wreaks havoc), there are engines and vehicles that allow us to travel cross country in hours or days, the ability to keep in touch with friends and families anywhere in the world with the touch of a keystroke. Many consider these incredible advancements and they potentially are. And they may also increase stress, depending on how they are used and your dependency on them. It is up to you to decide what stays and what goes so that you are ever moving toward simplicity and peace.

Innovations can be positive or negative just as electricity can pierce the darkness and provide light or burn and destroy. Thus, the debate is not about good or bad but about intention and force. Do we advance our technologies and science to expand consciousness and quality of life, or create struggle, competition, and stress? Can we align our efforts with universal principles that support life?

That is what we seek—to harmonize, to live life fully, to collaborate with instead of against others, and to align with the universe to enhance our existence. Opportunity is present in every moment. Let us be fully awake and alive. Therefore, instead of being swallowed up with all the great advancements, you pick and choose what makes sense for your lifestyle and supports your highest good. There are many people who love having their schedule on their phone. I personally like having a paper calendar. I receive great comfort in knowing that it will never crash, and it has no battery to go dead. I love the simplicity and having space to make copious notes. It is all about choosing what works best for you.

Activity: Take note of how much time you spend with technology. Are you doing practical things like withdrawing money from your bank account or are you spending hours on social media? Are you entertaining or educating yourself? Either is good if it aligns with your purpose. Pay attention to sitting too long, thinking too much, and when you need to walk away from your computer or phone. Make sure that you are using these advancements and they are not turning you into a techno robot with no ability to communicate person-to-person. How many hours do you spend on your computer or phone? How often to you move your body, take a walk, get into nature. Go to your heart and ask if there is balance. If not, make adjustments. Is there a better way to connect with your natural rhythm, entertain the need for movement, and be healthy? Pay attention; your answer will come.

Panic Attacks – No Problem

Every time you are tempted to react in the same old way, ask if you want to be a prisoner of the past or a pioneer of the future.
Deepak Chopra

A panic attack is a sign of being overwhelmed. The mind is trying to be in too many places at once. You might be driving home and then think of all the things you have to do tomorrow and all the things you did not complete today and soon you are in panic mode. The bottom line is that you can only be in one place at a time effectively. You cannot be in the present moment and be thinking about the past and the future. Your mind will go haywire and that is what a panic attack is—the mind going berserk—crazy.

There are folks who take drugs to stay calm but that is not addressing the issue with panic attacks. The real issue is that you are not in the present moment. It is fine to write a to-do list for tomorrow and include on it the things that were left over from today. It is not okay to get sucked into recrimination of what didn't happen and what should happen and then go into overwhelm because you are not in control of everything. No, it is true. You are not in control of everything. Accept it.

The key is to bring your mind back to the present moment and become tactile. For instance, I am sitting in this chair. It is a leather chair and I can feel the smoothness of the leather. I am facing this computer and it has a 20" screen. I am writing these words. I can feel the air in the room circulating and I can feel my feet on the floor. I can feel my lungs drawing in air and releasing it as I slow myself down. I can count slowly and calm myself into a peaceful state.

In other words, you can only be in one place at a time and that place *is* the present moment. That is the only moment you can experience at this time. It is the ONLY MOMENT YOU CAN INHABIT!!! You cannot relive yesterday and be at peace. You have no control over tomorrow (other than to make a to-do list). All you have is NOW.

Your power is in bringing your mind to the present moment. Be present in it. Look around. Feel your breath and observe your surroundings. Name everything in the room. There is the chair—it is green and has wooden arms and the upholstery has a nubby texture. There is a bookcase and it has a dozen books on the shelves. Some have black covers and others have brown or blue covers. There are even two red books. There is a rug on the floor, and it has a smooth texture and coordinates with the green chair. When I gaze outside the window, I can see a tree that is starting to turn fall colors and behind it there is a highway with many cars traveling to various destinations.

Continue to observe until your breathing gets calm and you are back to yourself. Think of it as looking out the window of your body to take note of all that is around you.

The truth is that you don't have to be everywhere or do everything. You don't have to be perfect and never make a mistake. These are stories you have told yourself. All you have to do is be in the present moment, breathing the air and quietly observing your circumstance. You don't even need a viewpoint or an opinion. What a great freedom to Just be present!

With practice and discipline, you can break a panic attack in a few minutes. Just remind yourself to become the observer without opinions or judgments. As you gently move your mind into calmness, you can peacefully decide your next move and do it with presence. A panic attack can even serve you when you use it to remind yourself that you cannot control everything or be everywhere at once. Then you can take decide where you want to focus and bring yourself back to the reality of this present moment! This is truly freedom!

The Purpose of Anxiety

*The important thing is NOT to stop questioning.
Curiosity has its own reason for existence.*

Particularly when life's responsibilities elevate beyond your capacity, anxiety can keep you aware of what matters most at any given time. Even though we often feel like the fellow juggling plates in the air, we can take a moment and realize that there is a plan B and C. There always is. Thus, anxiety can be a signal that there are adjustments to be made—perhaps a plan B or C to devise.

Anxiety is basically a sign that something we care about is at risk and we might not be able to protect it. Essentially, anxiety is grounded in a cause. Something isn't right.

We can alter our mood by changing our perspective and beliefs and that is important to know. Yet anxiety has another purpose. It signals a need to take a moment and examine priorities. Often, there is the thought of just getting rid of nervousness or restlessness, but perhaps a better plan is to first acknowledge that anxiety is a defense mechanism that is alerting us to a need to re-balance. Do you have an over-full schedule, or priorities that are out of balance, or you are placing too much pressure on yourself over issues that aren't worth it? Is it time to step back and examine where you are in life?

We have incredible natural instincts and intuition that can be trusted. We can heed that we are receiving an important message and there is wisdom in this innate system. Just as we would not hesitate to run from a tiger racing toward us, we can note that there is something of urgency to be addressed. Perhaps it is set to tear us limb from limb, but attention is needed to acknowledge and make adjustments.

Mindfulness expert John Kabat-Zinn describes our inner power in this way, *"like subterranean water or vast oil deposits, or minerals buried deep within the rock of a planet, we are talking here of interior resources deep within ourselves, innate to us as human beings, resources that can be tapped and utilized brought to the fore—such as our lifelong capacities for learning, for growing, for healing, and for transforming ourselves."*

We have enormous capacity and inner strength. Anxiety can serve as a tap on the shoulder, nudge from the universe, or a catalyst or motivating force that moves us to ultimate growth, success, and even peace. Stop and examine cause. Then decide what must happen next.

Adjusting Your View

The mind is a tool. The question is, do you use the tool or does the tool use you.
Zen Proverb

Most of us will miss out on life's big prizes…the Pulitzer, Nobel, Oscars, Tonys, Emmys, winning the Lottery. But there are many, more incredible prizes for which we're all eligible. For instance, have you ever looked at the night sky and felt complete wonder at its vastness; or merged so deeply with the rhythm and melody of music that your sense of self disappeared? Or have you felt magnetized by the light of love shining through a loved one's eyes; or drifted slowly awake and lain quietly embracing delicious restfulness before opening your eyes; or sat by a river, listening to its steady flow, and entered into stillness. These are life's small pleasures that transform an ordinary day to one of splendor, and a poor man into a person of extravagant means.

Each of these experiences exalts the soul and is readily available to anyone patiently embracing the moment. It is a matter of deliberateness—being willing to deliberately engage in life in a way, and, with the motive of transforming an ordinary experience to a memorable one.

The opportunity to share one's talents with the world seems like a wonderous experience and a chance to offer love in a grand way. But for singer, Carly Simon, who had incredible stage fright, it was terrifying. Before a performance, she would become nauseous and ill and even fainted at one of her concerts. Simon decided that she was not suited to be on stage because of her nerves. She routinely felt sick, her hands would sweat, and she couldn't sit still. She concluded that having this problem indicated that she was not meant to perform and actually stopped touring because of it.

Whitney Houston, on the other hand, knew that when her nerves were jangled, her hands were sweaty, and she couldn't sit still, she was ready to go on stage. She believed her nervousness made her mentally sharp and she felt pumped!

Both singers were anxious when going before an audience and demonstrated similar physical reactions, yet each interpreted them differently. Such it is with people. What exalts one person will disable another. In other words, are you willing to look fear in the face and deal with it or let it take you down?

If you are nervous with a new assignment or situation, it doesn't necessarily mean that you shouldn't go through with it. It could be a signal that something important is about to happen. It could be anticipation for a new door opening.

Before you give up, try adjusting your viewpoint. Excitement when starting a new venture can be expected. It is the way we meet challenge, face opportunity, and deal with the unknown. Acknowledge your excitement for what it is. It doesn't mean you should cancel the journey. New ventures lead to personal expansion and it makes life more interesting.

Therefore, when you find yourself in an anxious moment, stop and notice where you are? Shift your focus to the present moment and to your breath. That means notice the items or sites around you and start naming them. *There is a tree and some grass. I can smell the grass and watch the breeze blow through the tree.* Or, *I am driving and there are cars everywhere. There is a white Chevy and a black truck hauling gravel. I can feel my steering wheel and I can see the sun shining through the windshield.*

When you steady yourself and connect with the present moment, your mind stops racing and you begin to feel calmer. Next go to the place in your body where you can feel peace and breath into that space. (It might be your heart or your belly.) Breath at least five breaths while you fix your attention on your body. Put this exercise in your mental toolbox and it will be ready to use at any time. Bottomline, you are bringing your attention to the present moment and that is where all change happens. That is where all the fun happens too. From there, stabilize and center your attention.

I knew a woman who was depressed. One day, driving to work, she topped a hill and gazed upon a gorgeous scene. The horizon expanded before her with an incredible turquoise-blue sky and plump fluffy clouds. She was struck by the beauty and vastness of nature and entranced by brilliant arrays of flowers and massive trees that seemed to be crowned with sunshine. The immense stretch of branches opulently offering shade and comfort. As she registered this natural splendor, it occurred to her how unconscious and self-involved she had been. She wondered how much had she lost while depressed? Yet, throughout that time nature continued to radiate its grace and serenity.

These are the endless prizes we are offered. Are you willing to receive them? It requires a shift in perspective. Perhaps dropping a compulsion to self-doubt and letting go of negativism to open the door to deeper perception and appreciation.

Take a moment to look for the elegance of life and you will find it. Or, create a few of your own—pat yourself on the back, smile at someone, assume a welcoming stance to life. Go out of your way to be friendly to a neighbor. Or take time to gaze with wonderment at the moon and stars or listen to the melodious sounds of nature. Watch a crackling fire. Relax.

Enjoy the happiness of a cooing baby, the luxuriousness of a great meal, a gorgeous sunset, a bowl of hot soup, or a cold beer. These are the prizes that sooth anxiety and remind you that life is good.

There's no need fretting at losing out on life's illustrious awards. Appreciate its many joys instead. There are plenty of those to go around. Look around. What magic is happening right now that you would have missed if you weren't paying attention? Can you make a practice of noticing?

Anxiety is created in the mind. Situations do not cause stress. Your beliefs about them do. Jim sees a yard full of leaves and starts pressuring himself to rake it. Meanwhile, his next-door neighbor, Harry, observes the same sight, and, noting he has other priorities, walks right past without guilt or consternation. Jim can't release his obsession to clean up the mess. Harry has no pressure because he values his peace of mind above the yard waste.

Jim's belief that in order to be a good person, you must have a clean yard plagues him. Even though, he knows there is no time for yard work, he is burdened. Instead, he could focus on more compelling matters including self-nurturing.

This shift in perspective necessitates self-control and a redefinition of the prerequisites to being, a *good person*. Beliefs of this sort, and the ensuing pressure they instill, keep the mind disorganized. Contrarily, peace can be achieved by making it the priority. Let yourself off the hook. What's more important than mental harmony? Isn't that essential to accomplishing anything?

Putting peace at the top of your priority list makes sense. Many are unwilling to put this need on their list at all, much less at the top. *I'll get to my needs when everything else is finished."* It's no surprise then, when the day is over, you're still waiting your turn.

Start by dedicating an hour daily to shifting your paradigm of angst to peace. Do this by sitting quietly while contemplating beauty, peace, love, fun, everything working perfectly, etc. Your world will become calmer, brighter, and more hopeful. Simplicity speaks—leisurely walk, receive the sunshine (or rain), sit in reverie, fantasize a perfect life, read an inspiring book, smell the flowers, breathe deeply, write yourself a love note, meditate. The possibilities are endless.

Often, this kind of restructuring takes place when illness strikes in a family. Suddenly the messy yard, dusty furniture, or other important work loses significance. Health comes first. Guilt dissolves as tasks are ignored. The patient comes first (perhaps you are the patient). Don't wait for an emergency to include yourself on the priority list. Do anger, people pleasing, fretting about deadlines, and worry about the neighbors come before generating calmness? What are the unrealistic beliefs you hold that are interfering with serenity? How would you like to replace them?

To be in harmony, as the stream is to the rocks, is our task. It requires willingness, patience, and fortitude to shift your priorities and beliefs.

In our Western world, this can be a monumental accomplishment. Not so much in Eastern countries where silence is cultivated. Start by granting yourself permission to indulge yourself in a new way. In time you will get the hang of it and it will nourish you, even heal you. Stay in stillness for three days or a week, maybe three months. Remain until you have forgotten all the roles you play, and the ways you clothe yourself with identity and dysfunctional behaviors and beliefs. Stay until you become nothing, just quiet emptiness.

From this point, you can move into a deeper energy. Let the mind drift gently into experiencing a deeper sensation of life. Notice your breath. Feel it coming in and going out. Notice its texture, temperature, and rhythm. Feel your body organs function. And feel your spirit. Let it expand with each breath so that you are able to move beyond your physical self to feel the space you occupy. Then feel all space. Your mind will begin to change texture as you do this. It becomes softer, lighter, fuller. Stay in this space. No judgment, no anything, just being. You are stretching and becoming your true, authentic self.

The Journey from Anxiety to Peace

Relax and Get Real

You're not going to die. Here's the white-hot truth: if you go bankrupt, you'll still be okay. If you lose the gig, the lover, the house, you'll still be okay. If you sing off-key, get beat by the competition, have your heart shattered, get fired... it's not going to kill you. Ask anyone who's been through it.

Danielle LaPorte

Becoming your True Self is a matter of honesty and simplicity. When you are truly comfortable with yourself, the trappings of success can seem frivolous and unimportant. The feat is in recognizing that happiness is our natural state. When we don't confuse it with *things*, we can connect with an inner joy that reflects who we really are. It means taking time to relax.

Relaxing can mean taking time out of your day to *not be active* (be quiet) or it can indicate taking a break to experience mental space, let go of planning, busyness, analyzing and thinking. Shifting out of your analytical left-brain. Giving yourself time to move into emptiness (spaciousness) is deeply relaxing, healing, and rejuvenating. It is a form of meditation and brings you back to your center, to balance. This is doubly important for worrisome anxious people.

Action: First, get clear about what you want. Most people think about what they don't want. *"I don't want to be poor or bored,"* or *"I don't want to be alone."* Revise this list to indicate what you DO want. *"I want to make more money." "I desire more fun." "I want to spend more time building and enjoying my relationships with others."* Now you have something to work toward. Each of these items requires NEW actions. It's time to do something different. Start strategizing.

It is a matter of focusing forward rather than looking back. The past serves to educate you, but it is not a barometer of where you are to go. In fact, if you are reliving the past in your thinking, you are on a giant gerbil wheel going nowhere and becoming more and more stressed because you are working against nature. Nature is constantly evolving, changing, and expanding.

Monitor your thinking and speaking and you will easily recognize what your primary focus is and what you are projecting for the future. If you are talking about the debt you owe, you will continue to be in debt. If you speak about the excitement of a new project you have taken on, the future is being directed to excitement and newness. It is as easy as that. What do you want and what are you willing to do about it?

There was a woman who came to me for counseling because she was unhappy in her job. Her boss micromanaged and was always ready with negative, controlling behaviors and criticism. At first *Helen*, took her boss's behavior personally and felt terrible that she couldn't please her, but upon careful reflection she realized that her supervisor was threatened by Helen's skill with people and her ability to perform any task. When she recognized her boss's insecurity, she decided to reverse the dynamic between them, and she started complementing her boss.

The boss's reaction was instantaneous. She became friendlier and relaxed her determination to find fault. For Helen's part, she felt good that she could move beyond taking this interaction personally and glad she could see it for what it was. By looking beyond the surface dynamic, Helen recognized the real problem and was able to shift the energy and develop a happier work environment for both of them.

Helen's goal was peace of mind and that is what she created. In other words, she took responsibility for her own issue (taking things personally), made the necessary adjustment, and found peace.

You always have options. By taking responsibility for your life, you will discover ways to face change—adjust, move on, strategize, and expand.

Do something new every week. This will keep your mind open and agile. Condition yourself for expansion—try a new food, select a different style dress or hair, sing karaoke, take a Tai Chi class, learn to meditate. Introduce change in every area of your life.

Self-Expression – Find YOUR Way – Reduce Your Stress

Always be yourself, express yourself, have faith in yourself. Do not go out and look for a successful personality and duplicate it.

Bruce Lee

What is your true self? Think of yourself as a child—innocent, without preconception, and non-judgmental. You are eager, open and ready for life. You are excited and set to learn. You are focused in the present moment. What did you love to do as this child? What activity gave you the greatest joy? Your authentic self is love—no judgment, no worry or fretting. Just taking in life with innocence.

Deep relaxation requires letting go which is a challenge, an opportunity, and an art. You can develop this art by following the action steps in this manuscript.

Action: Before you respond to anyone or any situation, take a moment and ask yourself, what do I really FEEL about this? Then take time to construct your response. It is easy to get hooked into automatic reactions that don't truly reflect your real feelings or highest good. If you react without discrimination, you disconnect from your Self. Taking a moment will help you get REAL with yourself. (We have been taught many automatic reactions that do not serve our highest good. This is the time to recognize them. An example would be reacting with anger in traffic. Does it help? Will it make traffic move faster? Will you feel better about yourself by becoming angry?) What is your truth?

Along these lines, change your clothing and hairstyle to project a more relaxed attitude. I know a professional career counselor who wears sweat suits to the office and no one cares because they know she is genuine, caring and good at her work. She recognizes that she does her best work when relaxed and she follows her own cue.

You are that good too. You can let go of pretenses to care about things you don't really care about and engage in conversations that are of no interest and may even be boring. It can be as simple as changing the subject or leaving the conversation.

You can also make a ten-minute rule. I will listen for ten minutes and then I am out. Women often get stuck on being *nice,* and they end up doing things they don't want to do. Don't question your niceness. You are nice. Now be nice to yourself by being authentic. That means fill your time with activities that inspire you.

Henrietta was facing a divorce when I first met her. As she told me her story, she realized that she had completely changed when she got married. Instead of being the fun, playful, independent person she was before marriage, she had transformed into a serious, workaholic, mothering wife who lived off the remnants of her husband's attention. In other words, she had lost herself.

As it turned out, Scott (the husband) left her and their son in a huff because he *had enough!!* So, clearly, they both had issues, but this story is about Henrietta. Thus, after some self-examination, Henrietta revised her behavior and decided to reconnect with her creative self. This meant taking more time to do the things that inspired her and to find ways to fill her need for attention and love without depending on Scott. She basically became a new person. She learned how to be alone and to meditate. She got back into her creative pursuits. Scott, in the meantime, was a bit confused, yet intrigued.

To be clear, Henrietta got her strength back and this meant she did not fight with Scott over unimportant issues, nor did she interfere when he was being self-centered. What she did instead was become peaceful. Henrietta turned what appeared to be failure into self-actualization and reclaimed her self-esteem. It was a lovely conversion. And, by the way, Scott and Henrietta are still together and each one is feeling more fulfilled. Through Henrietta's actions and Scott's reactions their relationship has been transformed.

Have you lost the part of yourself that knows how to be happy? Have you become dependent on something or someone that diminishes your self-worth? Is there a way or action you can take to reclaim your enthusiasm?

You are Valuable – Acknowledge it!

Your value was set at the moment of creation. You cannot change it or minimize it. You are valuable.

Remind yourself of this daily. Talk to yourself out loud and affirm your value. Do not underestimate the power of your words and thoughts. In fact, how you talk to yourself is a make-it or break-it proposition when it comes to releasing struggle.

Just as you would not allow anyone to put you down, you are never permitted to speak negatively to yourself. Self-criticism and self-doubt hurt you, diminish your self-esteem and squash motivation.

If you believe you have low self-confidence, then your job is to build yourself up. Many people say horrible things to themselves. *How could you have done that; you are stupid; you are unlovable; you will never amount to anything.* These are lies and mis-creations. They are generated from an ego that demands control. Paying attention to ego railings is like having a giant thumb pressing down on you. If you listen to the negative rantings, you will never step out of your box or investigate your incredible potential.

I met a woman, "*Amelia,*" who was quite miserable and incredibly anxious. Upon her husband's death, she had taken over her his information technology business, and even though she was quite good at it, it did not make her heart sing.

She was essentially up the creek without a paddle with overwhelm and needed to make some changes or accept living an unfulfilled life. Many people are in the same predicament.

The question might be, does your heart have to sing at work? The answer needs to be YES! You spend a great deal of your life at work and you need to find joy and inspiration in what you do. If you don't you are going against natural flow, draining your innate resources, and depleting your life energy.

When you were born, you were alive with curiosity and wonder. You must find a way to ignite those same qualities in your work. That is how you engage your heart and soul and expand your talents. That is how you replace stress and anxiety with excitement and joy.

To continue the story, as *Amelia* spoke she told of her passion for art and how drawing the long slender lines of a cat felt ecstatic to her. It was clear, she had to get back into art. It was a way to wake up her True Self, raise her energy, and begin to value herself.

The thing that most people don't realize is that by devoting time to art, Amelia will ignite her authentic self and innate passion and she will find herself. By flaming her true self, she will know what she is to do with her IT business. She will get the answers she needs, regain valuable resources and life energy and, instead of living life in a confused state, she will have the clarity she needs to know who she is and what she wants.

In Amelia's case she ultimately needed to make a bold move and sell the business. That may seem radical on the surface but when you consider living life at half-mast and in a joyless state, it is not. Plus, there were employees to deal with and she did not want them to suffer for her lack of enthusiasm for the business. It is good to look at the whole picture because if you are not happy, there is a ripple effect and other people suffer the consequence.

It is true that each person is spiritually designed for something specific and even though Amelia fell into the IT business because of her desire to support her husband, it was not really HER business. Perhaps you have done the same thing and ended up in situations that did not fit or taken the easy path instead of looking for a synchronistic one.

Again, decide who you want to be and find a way to be it. Set a small goal for each day and complete it. It can be as easy as reading a chapter in a self-help book or starting a conversation with a new person each day. These mental shifts will ignite your self-esteem and give you another reason to pat yourself on the back. I know a fellow who loves himself for brushing his teeth twice a day. Yes, it can be that small.

Years ago, when I was entering the *singles* world, I enjoyed going to "singles" dances. In the beginning I did not know anyone, so I set a goal of speaking to at least five new people at each dance. *Hi, I'm Jean. Are you new here? How long have you been dancing? Etcetera.*

Nothing elaborate, right? What I discovered was that most people were grateful and relieved that someone spoke to them. They were way more tied in a knot than I was. (That may be true of you too.) It was easy, and I made a lot of friends. I thought of it as *giving friendship*.

When you consider meeting people as a *giving* action, it is fun. That doesn't mean that everyone will respond to you, but the vast majority will, and they'll love it, and the few who don't have issues you don't need to mess with. Try it; you'll like it!

By giving away friendship and love, you discover your value. Your energy shoots up to a high vibrational frequency and you accumulate wonderful experiences.

To live a stress-free life, you must know your strengths (everyone has them) and acknowledge your achievements. It is crucial. Each day there are challenges and no doubt you have experienced your share. Honoring this fact is important. Meeting challenge makes you strong. It is essential to honor this.

I am not suggesting shouting your strengths from rooftops. This is about using your inner dialogue (self-talk) to recognize and accept that you are a valuable person. This is how you begin feeling good about yourself. Give yourself credit. It is important!

Action: HAULT your mind when it partakes in negative self-talk. Refuse to give negativity credence. It is your mind—you get to say what goes on there. Mental discipline and toughness are key to releasing struggle so don't let your mind run on automatic pilot. Be vigilant about it. Remind yourself daily—hourly, in fact—*You are valuable!*

If you find yourself becoming overwhelmed with negative self-talk, move. Get out into nature and take a walk; breathe deeply. Take-action, such as cleaning out a closet or drawer. I know a fellow who cleans his refrigerator when he feels anxious and this action moves him out of his negative mindset. He calls is therapy and it works for him.

Once you have calmed down, write in a journal to expunge fears. Then follow up by expressing your desires, hopes and dreams. Clear your mind so that you remember that you are valuable. You are a unique piece in the universal puzzle that makes everything work. You are a valuable member of the universal orchestra and your instrument (expression) brings harmony to the whole. There is no one that can take your place.

Most people have been handed lots of negative programming as they grew up. The *grown up* (parents, teachers, everybody), not knowing the detrimental effects of put-downs or criticism, and being frustrated in their own lives, often and unknowingly, project their own programmed fear to their children. *Are you ever going to get it right? What's wrong with you? How could you be so stupid?* Or it could be subtle—a disappointed sigh or disdainful look. (You: *Oh, I let them down again! I'm not good enough. They don't' approve of me.*)

After a bit, we internalize the criticism and *they* don't have to say a word because the negative *program* is imprinted in our minds and it becomes a default button when things go badly. At this point, the program has become a neural pathway in your brain and presents as habitual negative chatter.

The question is: What to do about it? The answer is to reframe your limiting beliefs. Here are some steps to do that.

First, recognize when you have negative chatter. This can be as easy as noticing how you feel. If you feel angry, resentful, victimized, even bored, you have negative chatter.

Then notice your body. Where are you feeling tight? Clenched jaw, teeth grinding, knot in your stomach, lump in your throat, making a fist, tight shoulders or back? Your body never lies, and it will always reveal your thoughts.

Then, focus on one tight area and ask yourself, what have I been saying to myself? Do this as you release the tension. A great way to get in touch with your tension is to write about it. When you focus on your rigid jaw and ask yourself, what have I been thinking? Your brain dump can be, *I'm mad that I didn't get the promotion at work. Or, I feel ignored at parties. I think I got a raw deal with something.*

Brain dumping on paper is a great way to release negativity. You can keep a brain dump journal. When you have fully expunged the negativity, create a little ritual of tearing up the paper or throwing it in the fireplace. Some people go so far as to bury it. Your choice!

The next step is where things get interesting because it involves two parts. Part one is actually confronting the negativity straight on. For instance, *I always get passed over for promotion* or *things never turn out well for me* is addressed with a question—is that true? It is up to you to come up with evidence of validity. And, if you do find legitimate proof, the next question is, *why have I chosen to direct my thoughts that way?*

Now you are moving into *victim* territory. Living with victim mentality is highly destructive because you have set a life course for disaster and unhappiness. Truth: Victims are NEVER happy, and they are often extremely attached to their victim *whoa is me* life. It can be their claim to fame. I have actually seen people exit a positive, uplifting talk or workshop and immediately look for someone whom they could tell their *victim* story. That person needs to get real and possibly start a new hobby.

Years ago, I was in a corporate situation where it became obvious that there were folks who needed some personal growth assistance. Hence, we started a play-shop (as opposed to a workshop) to help them. One of the things we did was put people on trial and they had to defend their negative beliefs.

The whole thing was set up like a regular court room where the defendant had to present a case to support his negative self-opinion (present witnesses and documents or whatever evidence he had to support his case.) There was also a jury who would decide if his case was meritorious or flawed.

Thus, our first defendant had to defend his assertion that *"no one appreciates me"* or it could have been *"I can't do anything right."* You get the point. For instance, the idea that no one appreciates me was challenged by some folks who thanked the fellow for his help and acts of kindness.

It could have been that he held the door for someone or assisted with a project. As a result, the defendant had to re-think his position. Also, he began to more closely observe his interactions with people and found that his idea of no one appreciates me was flawed, and that is where the good stuff began, because at that point, he was obliged to change his thinking (and his story) and adopt a new way of perceiving himself, other people, and his situations.

One fellow had to concede his habit of indulging in pity parties. It was a great assertion because it helped him reformate his interpretation of events and interactions. In *"Ned's"* case he became more open and appreciative of himself and others and, in general, a happier person.

This "court" exercise was done with great fun, ardor, and honesty and was an effective tool to help folks make big shifts in their thinking. You get the point.

Once you have confronted your s*tory,* the second step is to make up a new one. Whereas the first part of the process is a brain dump, this part is a brain shift. You literally have to shift your mind to a positive possibility. If you don't do this, your mind automatically defaults to its old negative position. That is because you have invested many years into the *poor me* scenario and in some weird way it is comfortable (familiar). Thus, your new story will need a fair amount of reinforcement to become a neural pathway.

Therefore, if your old rendition is, *I'm not good enough,* start your new tune with, *I am more than good enough.* Think about your **positive attributes** such as kindness, gentleness, patience, generosity, being a good listening, keeping your word. (Everyone has positive qualities.)

Follow that with what life looks and feels like when you are more than good enough. Example: *people love to hang out with me.* Visualize people inviting you to join their party and laughing and having fun together. Visualize an active social life. Or, imagine people asking you for feedback or assistance at work and how good it feels to help out and how much they offer gratitude.

Another example: *Things never go my way.* The first step is to find the evidence. *Is this a true statement? Why do I want to hold on this idea? What is the payoff for me in believing this? What do I want my new story to be?*

Imagine a new scenario—serendipitous things happening all the time. People give you the right of way; you buy one item and receive two because today they have a special. Compliments fly at you from everyone! You get the idea.

The next very important step is to ask yourself if you really want this new positive life and if so, why? It is vital to have positive motivation to keep yourself moving. If your intent to change is not solid, you will put out a half-hearted effort and then say the exercise is futile.

Truth: it only works if you work it. If you receive a lot of rewards for having a sad story, you may not be ready to change. Answer truthfully, are you ready to release negative chatter and move to a more joyful experience?

Here is a summary of the process:

- Recognize the negative chatter. Note it.

- Feel the negative energy and determine where the tension is in your body.

- Challenge the disempowering chatter. Is it true? What is the truth?

- Decide if you want to keep the poor me story going forward or create a new one.

- Design a new story with positive feelings and affirming thoughts.

- I'm adding a bonus step—be grateful. Grateful you noticed the negative chatter, you challenged it, and you are creating and experiencing a new outcome.

Do this over and over until it becomes your default mechanism and soon the negative chatter will be gone, your life will be brighter, and you will be happier.

Comedian Groucho Marx must have gone through this process because these were his thoughts about starting his day.

Each morning when I open my eyes, I say to myself, 'I, not events, have the power to make me happy or unhappy today. I can choose which it shall be. Yesterday is dead; tomorrow hasn't arrived yet. I have just one day, today, and I'm going to be happy in it.

Another comedian, Tim Allen, embodies a person who started life in a self-destructive mind-set by selling cocaine. This act took place in his early twenties and led to spending more than two years in Federal prison. He readily admits that being funny kept him alive in prison and it served as a reality check. As a result, he decided to turn his life around and, just like that, he went from a *going no-where* path to picking himself up and doing what he was designed to do. He revived his stand-up comedy career and the rest is history because now he can name his venue and his televisions shows are hugely popular. If he can do it; you can do it!

and is followed by Winter's stillness. Plant life that vibrantly blossomed forth with brilliant arrays of color gently succumb to the slumber of Fall and dormancy of Winter. Work that inspired may fade so that you can graduate to the next experience and challenge. Relationships that were once vital pass away to make room for others that fit the current patterns of the life you live. We are always in motion.

Life is a great adventure and each person fulfills a mission as he navigates through a variety of experiences. Each is unique in his manner of processing and growing.

Motion is the power and instrument that makes this forward movement possible. Motion is a force that is not limited to the actions of a physical universe. It is also working from the level of thought, emotion, and spirit. (As in the case of Carrie.)

There is a fluidity about motion and change. You can see it easily as day passes into night or spring to summer. Yet it also presents in every other circumstance. You meet a person and there is an energy exchange which opens up a new possibility, which then sets up new circumstances that touches other lives and leads to movement in home, career, hobbies, community, and an even larger stage of exchange. You might complete an experience (a job or career) and become dormant in expressing a talent only to awaken to a completely new proficiency at a later date.

Change is a local symptom of a larger pattern of motion that is passing through your life, experience, and consciousness. We are ever growing with each change. Yet many people fear change. They believe they can control circumstances and never change. However, evolution and movement are the natural things of life.

The Journey from Anxiety to Peace

In this section we encourage surrender to change. Not in a way of helplessness or powerlessness, but in a cooperative effort, in a way to agree with movement toward the next step life offers, thus progressing along the path.

Whenever we are in battle with something, there is stress, and stress leads to anxiety. Nonetheless, when we step back to recognize that change is ongoing and natural, we give up the need to stand stagnant and obstruct movement. We are in the earth to advance our capabilities, to grow in resilience, understanding and compassion. Change is the vehicle through which growth happens.

When you become fixated with control and dominance, you can easily stymy personal progress. When you change as a result of restlessness, boredom, or fear, you may very well push forward out of rhythm, right timing, and what is to be.

What we seek is to make peace with change, to appreciate movement, and evolution. In other words, there is no standing still—you move, or life moves you. I've heard many people admit that they hated their jobs and were waiting to retire. They were basically living in fear and stress every day. The problem with such thinking is that if you are not in the right place (and work) and are unwilling to do something about it, the universe takes over and the job goes away, the company is bought, and your job eliminated, you are down-sized, or fired for some reason or other. In other words, you cannot remain in an inharmonious situation. If it does not fit with the natural harmony of the universe, it will end.

Your choice is to end it or be the victim of another kind of conclusion. As you adjust and cooperate with change as a natural phenomenon, you will be at peace and anxiety will not be problem. You change anxiety into excitement and flow with change. Everything in good time. Find compassion and forgiveness. In so doing, you are literally doing what masters have suggested for eons. *Forgive them for they know not what they do.* In other words, they don't understand that they hurt themselves more than they hurt anyone else. Perhaps their wounds do not allow introspection.

Rather than keeping yourself wound up, be radical and decide to be grateful for others presence in your life as it offers an opportunity for growth. This is like the Buddhist monk who when informed that he would be dealing with a very difficult teacher, said, *Oh, good; I can practice!* Oh, good, we can all practice!

It is true, life is nothing if not practice and each time you let go of struggle and anxiety, you grow a bit stronger and wiser. So, yes, practice. The truth is that nothing anyone does has anything to do with you. Each person is expressing his own level of development. The quicker you come to terms with that truth, the faster you grow and transform. In the process, the caterpillar (YOU) (become the butterfly!)

Live in Gratitude

*Gratitude is magnetic.
It draws everything good to you.*

Being grateful for the blessings life bestows is the most practical, high-minded thing anyone can do. Deciding to be appreciative and thankful for every wonderous thing in life immediately shifts you out of fear, anxiety, tension and angst. It is faster than a rocket taking off for the moon. The reason is that gratitude is a form of love and anxiety comes directly from fear. You cannot hold fear and love in your mind at the same time. Try it; you'll see! Therefore, by turning your mind to gratitude, which is love, you shift immediately out of fear and anxiety.

Gratitude is a high vibrational energy. It *lifts* your consciousness. On the contrary, fear is low vibrational energy and feels heavy in your body and mind. Shifting from low energy (fear) to high energy (gratitude) can be as easy as choosing to remember how blessed you are. This shift immediately adjusts your energy. Remember... the mind cannot focus on fear and love at the same time. They don't co-mingle. It is like trying to mix oil and water. It is one or the other. You choose!

Just to check this out, notice how you feel when you think of something scary (fearful). Example: *you don't' have enough money to pay the mortgage.* Ekk! The energy is heavy and constricted. You can feel the restriction in your body. Notice where you feel it. (Your heart; your gut?)

Now notice how you feel when you contemplate gratitude. Feel grateful for all the blessings in your life—relationships, children, car, sports team, sunshine, trees, food, water, whatever. The feeling of gratitude versus worry/anxiety is vastly different. Gratitude is light, expansive, and easy whereas worry is heavy, restrictive, and blocks flow.

Living in gratitude can be as easy as stopping midstream (at a moment's notice) and remembering the many gifts you have been given. That includes your talents, determination, friends, inventiveness, opportunities, air to breath, a home, everything. We have numerous

Jean Walters

Turning on Highest Intelligence

Cease trying to work everything out with your mind. It will get you nowhere. Live by intuition and inspiration and let your whole life be a Revelation.
Eileen Cady

As stated earlier, your highest intelligence is the heart and the heart and the right brain (creative center) work well together. The reason for this is that the heart is the intelligence of the present moment. It has no dictate to live in the past or to negative interpretations. Therefore, heart intelligence is your friend. It does not promote anxiety or worry. But it will provide answers and solutions if you choose to entertain them.

One way to connect with your creative brain is to cut the left brain (analytical, interpretive) out of your activities. That could be as simple as doing things for no practical reason—just because you want to. You're not doing them for money or to improve yourself, but simply for the sake of doing them.

Our logical mind wants a reason for doing things. It wants a cause-effect reason and a positive mapped-out result. *What is the positive result of doing this? What do I get out of this?* To move to your higher intelligence, do things because you want to, because you feel like it, and out of spontaneity. You can't plan for spontaneity, but you can decide in the moment to take a break, walk outside and breathe fresh air, take a drive, or do whatever strikes you. You can decide to have ice cream for dinner or call an old friend just because. You can follow your inclination for no particular reason.

You can also choose to breathe consciously. Try just one conscious breath while focusing on the body. Notice the breath going into the lungs and expanding the rib cage and belly. Notice the sensation of space and openness in the body. Perhaps you will let it release with a pleasurable *ahh*. You can become conscious and experience a natural body function in this way. By so doing, you avert the "structured" left-brain and move into your creative intelligence.

The point is that the more you shock your egoic mind by doing new things and following your intuitive mind and unbind your habitual thinking, the more you are able to open to your highest intelligence.

The last suggestion involves living in love. There is a whole section written on this idea. But the point simply is to love who you are, where you are, what you are doing, the environment, nature, animals, and everyone around you. Then you can add the greater world, politicians, movie stars, service people, writers (please), people in other countries and the entire world.

Lastly, moving to your higher mind is allowing new ideas and realizations to take root. Your mind is creative. When you open to new ideas, new methods, new techniques, and new ways, you are releasing stodginess, rigidity, stuckness and resistance.

Ask the universe for realizations about current circumstances, your relationships, how to do things, your next adventure. Ask and you shall receive. Keep asking and then create a receptive mind that new ideas can enter. Affirm, *I am open and receptive. I have new ideas and realizations all the time.*

The Wright brothers (bicycle mechanics) had the idea that they could make a flying machine—and they did! Thomas Edison believed he could record sound and invent a machine you could use to talk to someone in a distant place—and he did. These were realizations followed by activity. When you open your mind to right-brain, intuitive creativity, you will also can have realizations that will take you on adventures of discovery. Cultivate openness and you will remain young because young people live in spontaneity.

the rhythm and flow with it. Wholeness is achieved by going with the flow.

Open to Possibilities

Don't wait until everything is just right. It will never be perfect. There will always be challenges, obstacles, and less than perfect conditions. So what. Get started now. With each step you take, you will grow stronger and stronger, more and more skilled, more and more self-confident and more and more successful.

Mark Victor Hansen

Are you feeling stuck in your career, relationship, or some part of your life? If so, the question to ask is, *what have I been focused on?* In other words, if your mental, emotional focus is on how bad things are, that will continue to be your situation. If your attention is focused on how you've been wronged or unappreciated, you will continue to find yourself in similar situations. Or perhaps, your attention has been concentrated on opportunity, and the myriad ways to express and expand yourself. Guess what, that is what will show up in your life.

The truth is there are numerous opportunities to share, express, be active, have fun, make friends, start a new career, volunteer, or do anything else you want. The only limitation is YOU. As Albert Einstein said, *You are only limited by your imagination.* What are you allowing in your life? Where are you focusing your attention? Asking these questions and giving yourself time to answer them, will help you learn much and have the information you need to make wonderful changes.

There was a young man who held a high position at Microsoft. On his vacation he decided to hike through Peru. On his journey he came across a school where the children were eager to learn but had no books. He felt drawn to help them, and after getting all his friends to supply books, he determined to start a charity to assist children in poor areas have the educational tools they needed. As it turned out, he LOVED helping kids and followed his initial approach by creating a foundation to do just that, and his focus became a new career path for him.

Life is chocked full of possibilities, but you must be open to see and connect with them. If you are safe in your little comfort-cocoon, don't be shocked if nothing changes. People will complain *I don't like change. I'm uncomfortable with it.*

Guess what! Everything is changing all the time—so, *get* comfortable with it. Change is the order of the day. You can resist, but you will not come out on top!

Option: make life an adventure! Every time you confront a new experience or a new person, reach out and ask yourself, *what can I learn from this? How is this to expand me—my skills, knowledge, expression, and fun!* Then embrace it for the opportunity it offers.

Back to becoming unstuck.... If you are feeling stuck in any part of your life, there are steps you can take to get moving. In this example, I am focusing on career or work, but be aware that these steps apply to every happened because as he was returning home, his father came out to welcome him and told him he held no animosity or grievance. In fact, it was the father's great pleasure to give him his kingdom.

Wow! The bottom line is that it doesn't matter how many mistakes you make, there is always opportunity waiting for you. Forgive yourself because you are the one holding your feet to the fire. Let go of all the things you believe you did wrong because you are just clunking around trying to figure things out. Then forgive everyone else because they are doing the same thing.

It is true that people really are doing the best they know how to do. Hopefully as we continue to practice, we learn more and we get better. That is what forgiveness is all about. We are doing what we have been trained to do and as we fall, we learn to pick ourselves up and try again. Forgive yourself and everyone else.

Do you remember when you were in kindergarten and you sat in a little chair behind a tiny desk. Well, guess what, you now possess a beautiful adult body that no longer fits in that teeny desk or scenario. In the same way, trying to operate from old outmoded thought patterns that continually bring anguish no longer work either. In the same way, attaching to memories that bring pain need to go. They create anxiety and do not serve you.

Just because you belong to a family, social group, or tribe does not mean you have to allow the expectations and demands of others to be a source of unhappiness and stress. This is especially true if you want to express authentically and be at peace.

Other people are not the source of your discomfort. You are! You can label people as annoying, troublesome, or despicable and these are your projections. As you look at people differently—as wounded or lost—you will find forgiveness easy. Most of us have been handed a very inefficient playbook and we have been trying to make it work. A lot of it goes like this—these are the good people, and these are the bad people. It doesn't work.

Often, we busy ourselves deciding how others should be and when they are not that—respectful, considerate, kind, thoughtful—we get angry. They are not following the rules—your rules! Projecting your rules on to others and interpreting them through your standards is anxiety-provoking.

We really don't know what others have gone through to become the people they are, so categorizing in good and bad columns is simplistic and creates problems, particularly for you. Step back and look at each person objectively. For instance, Aunt Hannah has a knack for finding something wrong with everything and everybody. That is her quirk. It is not your job to change her. You can be disgruntled by her forbearance at finding fault, or you can see humor in it. You can become unnerved by Aunt Hannah's criticalness, or just observe it without judgment. It is a projection of her own unhappiness—the way she finds fault with herself. The key to happiness is taking care of your own business and letting others take care of theirs. In time you might find these strange behaviors humorous or even quaint.

The unalterable and ever effective way to experience peace is forgiveness. Each person is simply doing what they have been taught to do and what, in their mind, seems appropriate. Perhaps they have never questioned these tactics.

A wise, grounded person steps away from others' judgments and expectations and chooses instead to shower these same folks with parts of your life… relationships, friendship, abundance, health, fun—everything!

As Helen Keller put it: "Life is either an exciting adventure or nothing at all."

If your career generates anxiety and stress for you., you may need to make a change. If so, consider these steps to connect with a career that fits your personality and natural inclinations.

Steps:

1. Make a list of all your talents and abilities. Everything you've ever been good at. (Nurturing, organizing, connecting with people, baking a cake, selling an idea, climbing trees, giving orders, cleaning houses, technology, bossing people around, etc.)

2. Now, set the list aside—that list was for your analytical mind to recognize that you are multi-talented. You are setting it aside because it is time to let go of analysis, figuring things out, reasoning, and doing what you already know how to do. In this process you are opening your mind to the field of potentials and possibilities that can put these amazing talents to work in interesting and unique ways—perhaps ways you have never considered. In other words, as you set your list aside, you are getting your small (unimaginative) self out of the way so your greater mind can work.

3. Next, sit in a quiet place without distractions and pretend a door is opening to Spirit. You can imagine this door at your heart or your forehead (third eye). You are opening to the field of pure potentiality and limitless possibilities. To do this pretend you are in space—like an astronaut. You are not tethered or identified with any THING. Floating—in space. While you are doing this, your Higher Mind is working.

   Stay there until you feel stabilized/grounded. You are literally opening mental space for new possibilities to enter your life; you are allowing Spirit to take over and supply inspiration. Be still and spacious and It will come forth. Do this over and over and your next step will be revealed. (You can practice this form of meditation over many days or weeks.) Be patient; stay open.

   Your next action could be anything—meeting a certain person, taking a class, joining a *meetup social group*, moving your home, reconnecting with an old friend, putting an ad in the paper, calling to inquire about a position, joining Toastmasters, taking a leap of faith.

   One gal was a corporate senior technology specialist and decided to quit her job (that was sucking her life) so that she could deliver pizzas at night and write a book during the day. This radical change allowed her to move into her creativity. She wrote two novels, created music, and became an amazing portrait artist.

   Another woman quit an office job that was killing her and became a trapeze artist. In her transition, she became alive and purposeful. So, who knows… anything is possible!!

4. Visualize the kind of activity that would be fun to call work. Recognize that this activity is your True expression and it will generate wages/income. Do NOT concern yourself with HOW it will manifest or when, or who, or any other detail. Just enter this picture and FEEL the excitement and fun. Give this exercise 5 minutes. You can do this twice a day. Keep visualizing because each time you do, you intensify and densify the energy of your new path. Again, have fun, and don't concern yourself with timing, when, where or who. That is the Universe's job, not yours.

5. Give thanks, let go, and get on with your day and do what is in front of you to do. Keep your mind clear by enjoying your present work. That means no complaining, blaming, or other negative energy. It gets in the way and creates a new picture, which overrides your visualized idea.

6. Do these steps again tomorrow and the next day. Spirit follows as the mind directs. If you are clear in your intention, opportunities are revealed. If you are urged to put your application in at a particular place, do it. If you feel pulled to do something you have never done before, good! Do it! Pay attention and you will be guided. Follow it without question or hesitation.

With just a little willingness on your part, miracles happen. Stay focused and have fun!

The Journey from Anxiety to Peace

To Create Ease Forgive Yourself and Everyone Else

The weak can never forgive.
Forgiveness is the attribute of the strong.
Mahatma Gandhi

An incredible truth is that people think they can get through life without making mistakes and yet the whole experience of life is trial and error. No one has been handed a manual on how to get through life without getting bruised. So, why is it that we can be so hard on ourselves when we misstep? Life on earth is a mistake-making proposition. It is the place where we learn and figure things out. If we already knew all this stuff, we wouldn't even be hanging out here at all. Thus, the key to being happy is to accept our slip-ups and blunders as part of the journey and keep motoring on. Just as you don't criticize a baby for getting up and falling down as he learns to walk, you don't down yourself for the same thing. We are all learning how to walk.

Do you remember the story of the Prodigal son? He left his wealthy father's house and went out into the world, blew his inheritance on gambling and various questionable activities, hung with an unsavory crowd, and ended up eating garbage from the pig's trough. We might say that he basically screwed up. Yet it was after he hit bottom that he woke up to the fact that he could return home to a loving father, a beautiful home and even if he were to live out his days as a servant in his father's house, it would be a good life. And that is when the magic

V. Flow with Life

Motion and Change

Nothing diminishes anxiety faster than action.
Walter Anderson

In this section, we are to look at life from a higher dimension and appreciate the movement and rhythm of change for its higher purpose in developing individual potential and creativity.

Here is an example: Carrie was having trouble making her quota in her sales job. So, she did two things. First, she quit paying attention to her quota because it made her nervous. Second, she decided to pay attention to her intuition. Thus, it happened that one day she woke up with the idea of visiting a customer in a small town quite a distance away. Often in the past, she ignored these impulses. But on this day, she decided to listen to the urge and follow it. Therefore, she traveled to meet the customer and present some new products that could help the customer in his business. The interesting thing is that when she arrived she discovered that this manufacturer had been pondering innovative ways to move his business forward. Thus, Carrie's timing was impeccable. And so, it happened that she made a great connection, helped the customer accomplish his objectives, and ended up superseding her quota.

The bottom line is that Carrie never stopped listening to her intuition because she now knew that it always led her to the fruition of her intention, be it sales, or anything else. She knew that whatever the need, there was always a way to meet it. By changing her focus, Carrie was changed forever.

Psychologist, Mihaly Csikszentmihalyi, has termed this sense of rhythm (when we follow our heart or intuition) flow. It also applies when we are doing what we love, what synchronizes with who we are, we are in rhythm and flow. He thinks of it as being in a zone where the person is totally absorbed in what he is doing, completely involved in the activity for its own sake, each thought and activity naturally proceeds from the previous one. Your whole being is involved and you are using your abilities to the utmost. We can use change in this way—as a moment shifting us step by step to our right place and correct endeavor. Just like John was moved to fulfilling his desire to be a business owner.

It is true that change is the only constant. You cannot stop it or interfere with it. It is on-going and occurring every minute all the time. What you can do is learn to deal with it appropriately so that you are not creating anxiety around change. You can learn to flow with it.

Think of all the ways we accept change. Day turns to evening and then to night. Stars and planets that were previously invisible, pop out in a diamond studded sky. Spring blossoms to life, then morphs to the busyness of Summer. Fall arrives with a sense of slowing down, nesting, advantages and often we forget to be grateful. Yet this can be one of the easiest, most powerful practices to add to your toolbox. Gratitude on awakening, gratitude throughout the day, gratitude when you go to bed. Investing fully in gratitude will change your life—instantly!

Thus, imagine you are stuck in heavy traffic that seems to go nowhere and you are becoming tense and nervous and then you remember that you have the freedom to drive, to own a car, to call ahead and let colleagues know you are running late. Many people, cultures, nations have none of these advances

There are many narratives relative to gratitude in the Bible. Luke tells the story of Jesus passing through a village in Samaria when he encounters a group of ten men who suffer from leprosy. The men cried out to Jesus to have mercy on them to which Jesus responded by healing them. He then instructed them to show themselves to the local priests to be ceremonially cleansed.

The men did as they were instructed and went their separate ways except for one of them. No doubt they were excited to celebrate their healing and rejoin society and possibly the tenth man had similar plans, but he wanted to do something else first.

As Luke tells it, he returned to Jesus and in a loud voice glorified God and fell down at Jesus' feet giving him thanks. Jesus was moved by this man's heartfelt determination to go the extra mile to express gratitude, and because of his action, the man was able to connect with the master in a profound way. That profound connection is what occurs for anyone who chooses to live in gratitude.

When you pray as though you have already received that which you request, you are living in gratitude. Gratitude is a powerful principle that draws to you great good. It keeps you in an open, receptive mental state and allows increased blessings to flow in your life. In gratitude there is NO anxiety or worry.

Exercise: Before you start your day, spend a few minutes giving thanks. That includes gratitude for everything planned for the day, all miracles yet to happen, and your everyday blessings. Infuse every event, person and activity with gratitude. At the end of every day, do it again. Perhaps you can start a gratitude journal and write down at least five things for which you are grateful from your day. This action will keep your attention in a high energy state AND gratitude eliminates anxiety.

Let go by Laughing More!!

Humor is the healing balm of angels.

As you let go of worry and projected outcomes, you will be able to detach enough to see the silliness of life. Enlightened beings are just that—light. Cultivate humor as it keeps your energy and mental state elevated. This is how you create mental spaciousness.

Choosing a lighter approach means your capacity to accept the twists and turns life throws your way graciously increases. You more readily understand that the world will not end if you don't get your way or get bound up and take yourself (ego) too seriously. In fact lightness increases your chances of achieving the results you desire. Additionally, you free up time because guarding your fragile ego, lest it be wounded, is a time-consuming proposition. It can keep you endlessly bogged down and continually upset.

A vulnerable ego is a setup for pain and anxiety. You don't want to waste time worrying about things over which you have no control. Instead find a way to laugh at the past (it was an adventure), face the future (it is full of possibilities), and push on.

Laughter has been proven to heal ailments because it elevates your energy. Laughing allows tension, depression and suppressed negativity associated with the past to be released, at least temporarily. Humor helps you see another side to life and form a new perspective. The idea is to let go of heaviness, intensity, and pettiness. You may even reach the point of laughing at yourself. Yay!

Every situation has a humorous side. If you can detach enough to become an observer of life, you will find the humor. Become the observer. Every comedian started his career by finding humor is his dysfunctional life. He talks about it, makes fun of it, and he heals from it. We can do that. When humor is in the foreground, anxiety is relegated to the background.

Here are some ways humor can help you:

- Form a stronger bond with other people. Laughter connects people.

- Smooth over differences. It will help you deal with even the most sensitive issues, politics, sex, in laws, whatever.

- Diffuse tension and resolve disagreements.

- Overcome problems and setbacks. Humor gives you resilience and the ability to manage adversity.

- Put things in perspective. Humor helps you reframe a situation. What could seem overwhelming immediately reduces in size with humor.

- Be more creative. Humor lightens your mood and inspires playfulness.

Rodney Dangerfield is considered the greatest stand-up comedian. Few people know that he developed his humour to counter depression. His famous line, *I get no respect,* was taken from his life. Yet, nothing gave him greater pleasure then igniting an audience with laughter. It is possible that many comedians use the same motivation to lift their moods.

Step back and instead of focusing on how bad things are and your tendency is to worry, train yourself to see absurdity. Observe the way people manipulate each other, rationalize to make themselves right, blame others, fight over insignificant things, or get carried away with details while missing the point. You have no control over others' actions and they surely bear the consequences of them, so you may as well notice and enjoy the show. It is a show!!

One of the biggest stories on using humor and laughter as a way to heal illness, and anxiety is offered by journalist, Norman Cousins, who experienced a case of crippling connective tissue disease in 1964. In his effort to heal his condition, Cousins researched the biochemistry of human emotions, which he believed were the key to success in fighting

Managing the mind and letting go of anxiety takes time and practice and it is doable. The methods, techniques and meditation outlined in this book work. They require practice and they will help you. Practice makes perfect and living a life of peace is worth the effort. It can be accomplished.

Use the tools in this book and you will discover methods that work well for you. If you get to a place of struggle, randomly open the book and read whatever principle is outlined there. Your subconscious mind will direct you to what is needed and no matter what, don't give up but stay with it.

You were designed in love and love is your essence and core. You will find your way back to love and when you do you will feel as though you have returned home. Anxiety disappears; peace returns. May you enjoy the journey.

Acknowledgments

Life is a journey and there are many people along the way that inspire, challenge, teach, and encourage. I do not take any of them for granted and I know beyond knowing that each in his own way have helped me become the person I am today and achieve the peace that I possess.

I acknowledge my mother, Helen Vosbrink Davenport, as my great inspirator and teacher. She is the reason behind this book and my journey from anxiety to peace. In her the universe supplied me with a dedicated parent and a wonderful muse. My dad, James Blaine Davenport, was the steadying force in our household. I acknowledge him for always being present and dependable. He was a rock!

I also acknowledge all the people I have worked with over my 40-year career that have supplied content for this book. Each has inspired me in their quest for improvement and peace. Some will find your story offered in these pages. I feel privileged to have been allowed to know you and serve you on your path to enlightenment.

Cathy Davis is a talented designer and creates beautiful book covers, among other things. Collaborating with her has been a gift. Anne Cote is my awesome editor. She is an absolute joy to work with. I acknowledge my book coach, Scott Allen. He led me through the process of publishing with pearls of wisdom and sage advice. He is a master at keeping it simple. I feel blessed.

The Journey from Anxiety to Peace

Thank you to my students, clients, and readers. You are my everyday inspiration. May you find a kernel of truth in this book and may it brighten your life.

Thank you for reading *The Journey from Anxiety to Peace: Practical Steps to Handle Fear, Embrace Struggle, and Eliminate Worry to Become Happy and Free*

Can you help get the word out about this book by writing a review? Amazon.com loves reviews and endorses books that have them. Please go to Amazon.com and put the name of this book and author in the search box and click on review or stars to write your review. Was there a main point or message you received from this book? Please let me know. I am eternally grateful for your help!!! Jean Walters

Would you opt in to hear about the next book? You can go to my website: www.spiritualtransformation.com and sign up for my newsletter (front page) and I will keep you in touch with the latest happenings and specials. Thank you, again for staying in touch.

Jean Walters, DM, DD, CRT

www.spiritualformation.com
jean@spiritualtransformation.com

About the Author

Jean Walters has been at the forefront in the movement for personal transformation, clarity and truth for over 40 years. Through her writings, consulting, coaching, and Akashic Record Readings for people all over the world, she has been a consistent source of light, clarity and inspiration. Jean's intention and commitment to deepest truth have brought her to share her wisdom and guidance to tens of thousands of clients and students.

As a leading authority on metaphysics, she promotes deep spiritual connection and enlightenment. She has authored articles and columns in major newspapers and magazines all over the United States and is a best-selling author on Amazon.com. Her books include:

- Set Yourself Free: Live the Life YOU were Meant to Live!

- Be Outrageous: Do the Impossible – Others Have and You can too! (Find Your Passion)

- The Power of KNOWING: Eight Step Guide to Open your Intuitive Channel and Live in Highest Consciousness

- Dreams and the Symbology of Life, soon to be transformed into The Mystery and Magic of Dreams

Walters has designed and presented classes and workshops on empowerment, meditation, building communication skills, universal laws, dreams interpretation, strengthening intuition, and creating spiritual connection for many organizations, colleges, universities, spiritual groups, and businesses. She continues to offer her services to empower others.

She is the recipient of The Marquis Who's Who Lifetime Achievement Award and listed in Who's Who 35 times. You can find her books on Amazon.com

From her office in Saint Louis, Missouri, she works with people around the world as a Transformational Coach and Akashic Record reader. She has performed over 35,000 readings with the emphasis on providing insight regarding personal growth, life purpose, strengthening relationships, and moving through obstacles. She has been presented with *Best Psychic in Saint Louis Award* for six years.

Walters' mission is to lead people to the Light – to encourage, guide and assist others to live freely and express from their Highest Selves. You can reach her through her website.

Jean Walters, DM, DD, CRT

www.spiritualtransformation.com

eyes. You can feel his/her serenity and you easily let go and dissolve into bliss.

He/she reaches his hands out to you and you give him yours and as you touch you feel yourself lifted. You feel the connection, a deep soul connection—a heart connection.

As you relax and open up, you feel yourself letting go of everything, and you sense a transmission of energy coming to you from the master. He is speaking to you energetically. Listen carefully. Listen with your heart. You might hear his message as a symbol, a sound, words, a song, or an answer that you have needed. Perhaps you are simply experiencing his essence. It is enough.

When this message has been delivered, you will see a smile of approval crossing his face and soon his form begins to fade, and you will know that even though he is departing now, he will return again soon. Allow yourself to sit quietly absorbing the joy of this encounter.

Keep this feeling of peace with you as you slowly begin to bring your attention back to your physical form. Feel your feet touching the earth and connecting as a tree is rooted to the ground. And when you are ready, feel yourself occupied in your body and take a deep breath to bring yourself fully back to the present moment. Gently open your eyes. When you are ready, write down the message you have received.

Choices and Conclusion

For one who has conquered the mind, the mind is the best of friends, but for one who has failed to do so, his mind will remain his greatest enemy.
Bhagavad Gita

There are some interesting statistics regarding generalized anxiety disorder. Did you know that anxiety is behind many major illnesses: headaches, irritable bowel syndrome, sleep disorders, substance use disorder, chronic pain, fibromyalgia to name a few? When it comes to anxiety disorder in adults, it is reported that an estimated 6.8 million adults are affected during a year or 3.1% of the population of the United States.

Globally around 4% of people experience generalized anxiety disorder at some point in their lives and the median age of onset is 31 years old, although symptoms may start much earlier and become gradually pronounced. Depression is the most common symptom of Anxiety Disorder.

Fear and anxiety create struggle and the dangerous mental condition behind serious illness. They play out in the nervous system and, if they are not dealt with, can ruin your life. Yet fear and anxiety can be managed, and even eliminated. The methods in this book address

anxiety and instruct in mental practices that can bring an end to suffering.

The mind is the creator. Everything can be changed by proper mental focus and discipline. Stressful thoughts such as hate, resentment, anger, and fear are behind this nervous state. Learning to manage your thoughts and where and how you focus your mind is the solution.

As you assume more and more mental control you develop the ability to withdraw attention from the sensory world to experience a deeper reality where fear does not exist. It takes practice, endurance and purposefulness to keep moving forward and experience a shift in perspective, awareness and openness. Yet, with all progress, there is profound welcoming and appreciation.

There is a peaceful space within every person. We are all made in the image and likeness of God. That means we are all made of the same stuff. We are harmony and we are love. Yet, because we have not been trained to believe this, there is effort involved in reverting back to our original state of innocence and love.

We can access this space through quiet contemplation, meditation, and developed observation skills. Just because a thought flies through your mind does not mean you have to engage in that thought. Ideas, beliefs, and thoughts come and go like a breeze through a tree. You can observe a thought and release it in the same way that the tree does not obstruct the breeze. It does not hold on to the wind and you don't have to invest in every thought. Thus, when negative thoughts appear, train to let them go.

When you feel a breeze, you don't have to dramatize it into a hurricane or tornado. It can be a breeze. A thought can be a thought that is noted and released—nothing more.

That is the value of mental discipline. You can also notice a stressful thought and redirect your mind to something pleasant. It is your mind. Ultimately, it is up to you to choose your thoughts.

Recently someone told me that she was rudely treated at the airport, where she was essentially told that she had lied about purchasing a pass-through ticket. (She had not lied.) At the time, she was enraged at this treatment and started to protest, and then she redirected herself to let go of the anger she was feeling, as it felt awful to be so mad. Per her own determined effort, within minutes she had returned to a happier state. At the time, she was traveling to visit her daughter and grandchildren and she wanted to focus on her happy journey and her loving family. She used her training to get centered and choose peaceful thoughts. Per her own report, *she felt so much better being happy.*

We are living in a period of great transformation. Everywhere you look there are new methods for attaining old objectives. Technology has opened a vast window of exploration and new, inventive possibilities show up every day. For this reason, we must be alert to the potential for overwhelm and anxiety and be ever on guard to stay centered in the peace we have chosen.

The ego will always promote fear-based thinking because that is how it controls. Hence, each individual is vested with deciding where he wants to place his attention. This is a discipline and it will take repetition and time to perfect and the results are always dynamic, powerful, and worthwhile.

environment to permit reception. Your highest function is to channel this flow.

Take time daily to contemplate what you are doing and where you are going. Choose to move slowly. Be reasonable, not demanding, in your expectations of self and others. Listen to beautiful music, observe art and inhale the freshness of flowers. Be quiet. Only then, do you have the choice to be on or off life's treadmill.

When you are operating in natural rhythm, your awareness of self and the world, as well as your potential for movement, grace and peace are heightened.

Activity: Each day walk in nature or go to a place of beauty—an art gallery or exhibit, a body of water, a garden. As you walk, release your *thinking/analyzing* mind and move into your heart to feel the essence of your surroundings. It might help to put your hand over your heart to bring your focus there. As you do this, you relax deeply. Add some deep breaths to complete the sensation of serenity. This becomes a time of healing and self-nurturing and you are refreshed as you move back into your world of *doing*

Second: Reframe Your Mind – Make Love Your Center

Darkness cannot drive out darkness; only light can do that. Hate cannot drive out hate: only love can do that.

Love is your natural essence and core. If and when you move away from understanding this, the odds are that you are entertaining fear and buying into a mental construct of lack and limitation. Yet those ideas don't really change anything because love continues to be the quintessential principle out of which everything is made.

When God decreed, *let there be Light and there was Light and he called it good,* the kernel of life (Light), from which you (we) emerged, was established.

Since that declaration there has not been a moment that your basic essence has not been alive in love. Over eons, you potentially added layers of mental activity and dense material substance to this original manifestation, but you have not changed the truth of your being. You are Light and you are Love. (Light and love being the same creation.)

When we examine the structural world with the eyes of love, we observe the mental constructs of our creative mind. In other words, whatever we cast our gaze upon, has been projected from our own essence.

We know this to be true because one person can look at a tree and see a marvel of nature—unlimited leaves, an immense structure spouted from a tiny seed, a towering assembly of trunk, roots, branches and leaves growing in strength and stability over many years. At the same time, another person will gaze upon a tree and register its need for pruning, the hundreds of leaves that have fallen to the ground waiting to be raked and fear a potential hazard of it collapsing on his house. Each individual perceives what has meaning for himself.

All the while, the tree stands sturdy against the wind, providing shade, and possibly limitless flowers or fruit. It continues on without worry or concern over what will happen next. In fact, whatever the next moment brings is accepted fully. If a wind causes a branch to break and fall to illness. Even though, he was informed that he had one chance in 500 of recovery, Cousins decided to develop his own recovery program, which included self-induced bouts of laughter brought on by the televisions show, *Candid Camera* and various comedic films. He later detailed his recovery and what he termed *laugh therapy* in his book *Anatomy of an Illness as Perceived by the Patient*. The bottom line is that he healed from his illness.

We can all attest to the healing effects of laughter. No doubt everyone can say he feels better after a good bout of laughter. It is a great way to let go of struggle and heaviness and should be included as a daily therapy to bring us back into balance.

To really let go, try to see a bigger picture of life. What is really going on? Keeping the purpose of an event in your focus helps you recognize silly actions or reactions—even your own. That is when you have power to change.

People often get waylaid on their journey and forget their purpose. That is when laughter can set you straight to continue on. We need it; it is a healing balm.

Enjoy life; it keeps you healthy. How many happy people have you seen with serious illnesses? I'm not referring to clowns who crack jokes to cover insecure egos, but well-adjusted individuals who don't go off the deep end over inconsequential concerns. They maintain clarity and perspective and play life as a game. Sometimes it is a party, other times a circus, a drama, or a mystery. Always it is entertaining and educational.

Children are masters at having fun and enjoying life. Observe them. If they get upset over something, within five minutes they have released and moved on to something else. In other words, they don't keep themselves upset and ruminating.

There is an art to taking life lightly. It is good to address this skill as an important tool because laughter and joy are health-producing stimulants. Joy increases circulation; laughter shakes your body, loosening and soothing tense nerves and muscles. Fun allows body parts to return to their natural rhythm and functioning capabilities. There is no muscular resistance to inhibit natural flow and processes. Make laughter a therapy and a way of life.

When you exist in high energy, your body innately shifts to its natural rhythm. Healing occurs; you can breathe more deeply. You let go and relax. Your mind is in natural flow.

Action: Look for the silly side of every situation. It is there. It can be the way people overreact to things. Like running out to buy bread and milk every time there is a *bad weather* report. Or, how someone gets bummed if things don't go their way and act like a little child, even though there is clearly a better way.

When a setback occurs, instead of jumping to conclusions, making up a story, and reacting badly, take time to step back and view it objectively. (How would you see this if it were someone else's situation?) When you create a little breathing space, a new direction or alternative method will present itself. Locking down options limits you and you really are not limited. Laughing keeps your spirit free, open and flexible.

Laugh at your own foibles—the way you have to follow a certain routine. Then, of course, there is *Laugh Yoga,* attending inner child workshops, funny movies, and setting up a weekly play day. No one outgrows the need for play. On this day take yourself on a date and do the ground, a new branch grows in its stead. The spirit of the tree does not change or falter. The tree was created in love and continues to stand firm in it. Thus, nature carries on undisturbed according to the spiritual matrix that makes up its being.

Can we look in beauty at the tree, the leaves, trunk and roots? Can we observe each person as a unique combination of qualities, skills, and potentials—each formed in a unique pattern (like snowflakes)?

Is there one right way to be? No! Yet as we gaze, we can believe there is and reject the various forms and designs before us.

What is love? It is accepting "what is" without resistance. By seeing the beauty of each being and creation, we move to the heart and become love. Love does not decide right and wrong but accepts conditions as they are. A twisted tree, a disabled body, a storm (internal or external) can be loved.

Becoming love means to keep yourself in the present moment. That means when your mind wants to race ahead or live in the past, you focus instead in the present. It means accepting things as they appear to be while working to change that which is inappropriate or unsuitable. It means recognizing the forces at play as they unfold in present moment events. (Hating or resisting *what is* creates chaos and fear.)

Accepting events and people as they have evolved gives us a chance to look at ourselves and ask, *what in me needs to change?* As we receive the answer, we face the opportunity of growth—expansion in love and in being what and who we want to become. It is a process and a journey. We accept the long-term vision and work with it day-by-day.

Here is the activity: For ten minutes in the morning, look at the world in wonderment and the openness of a child. No judgments—just observe the miracle of it all. In the afternoon do another ten minutes of gazing at the world and situations in the world without judgment, but with a sense of amazement as to how universal energy has formulated into this or that situation or event.

If you choose to, do another ten minutes in the evening. Look with admiration at all the different sizes, shapes, and expressions of people. No judgment. Just let your mind broaden into a sense of wonderment and amazement. As you do this exercise, your anxious mind—ego—will fight to judge. Don't let it. When you feel yourself moving toward judgment, bring yourself back to awe.)

Third: Meditation as a Mental Discipline to Erase Anxiety

Meditation is not just a rest or retreat from the turmoil of the stream or the impurity of the world. It is a way of being the stream, so that one can be at home in both the white water and the eddies.

Gary Snyder, Just One Breath

Meditation is a mental discipline that trains your will. If achieving peace is a real goal, meditation is a necessary technique that will take you there.

In meditation practice you focus on stillness (silence/ emptiness) to achieve deep relaxation. In time, as calmness becomes natural, you are able to deepen your process and connect with your highest consciousness. You start by relaxing the physical body. You may do this by tensing and relaxing your muscles and then taking several full breaths. With each breath, think of relaxing a little bit more.

There is an American Indian story about two wolves. Each person has two wolves inside. One is a good wolf and the other a bad wolf. That means that the good wolf is encouraging, empowering, and positive and the bad wolf is angry, negative, and disempowering. Whichever wolf you feed becomes the dominant wolf. Which wolf are you feeding?

I have introduced this story (metaphor) so that you will consciously choose the wolf (part of you) you want to feed. Meditation feeds your empowered self. As you relax your body, mind, and emotions, you are to focus on the quality of openness or emptiness.

You do this by letting go of earthly concerns and visualizing a beautiful internal Light around your heart. This Light dazzles with brilliance and we come to realize that this light is LOVE. As you gaze at it, an inner space of serenity opens. Keep your focus on this stillness, peace, and inner Light for ten minutes.

Holding your attention in this deep inner space for a few minutes every day will produce amazing changes. With regular practice, you will feel stronger, more stable, healthier, and more optimistic. You will have greater insight, intuition, and objectivity and your sense of deepest connection will expand.

There are many health benefits to meditation. Medical science has endorsed it as a tool for overcoming stress, lowering blood pressure, reducing worry, and creating an overall sense of well-being. Successful people meditate for clarity.

Meditation to relax and connect with your Inner Guide

Quiet the mind, and the soul will speak.
Ma Jaya Sati Bhagavati

Sit in a straight-backed chair with your feet on the floor and your head up. Relax your body and begin to take in several deep breaths. With each breathe imagine your body and mind relaxing. Your body releases tension like water flowing out and your mind becomes clear like a lake that is quiet and absent of ripples.

As your mind becomes as clear as a mirror, shift your attention to imagine a clear open landscape. A beautiful grassy field as far as the eye can see. Perhaps there are flowers, shrubs and trees and you can feel a sense of calm and stillness.

As you quiet your mind, you begin to see a light emerging and growing in the field. As this brilliant light approaches it crystallizes into a beautiful Light Being and then a person—an enlightened master or guide.

As the master approaches, you notice a big smile on his/her face and the feeling of excitement grows. Soon you are gazing into each other's and those individuals taking part in a mindfulness group had a reduced level of a bio-markers for inflammation linked to disease such as diabetes, arthritis, and cancer.

This research points to the potential of cultivating inner calm and recognizes that it is the antidote to anxiety. Just as you would train your body to run a marathon, you must train your mind to be peaceful. You can do it. It is important.

By working with the principles and techniques outlined in this book you will develop a mental default system that can carry you through challenges, and you will develop the mental fortitude of a phoenix rising from the ashes of completed experiences. It is doable and it is within your reach.

If at any time you get stuck, randomly open this book and take in whatever principle is before you. It will refresh your resolve. In time you will have conquered fear and opened the door(awareness) to a new you and you will know that the effort was well served.

We can live in such a way as to fixate so much on the outer world and the challenges therein that we lose connection to our inner sanctuary and that is a price too high to pay. In other words, sometimes things have to go away (dissolve, be destroyed) so that one can focus on important matters. This is evolution and we must embrace it.

What are your values? People get stirred up over a bad monetary investment. Yet, if their child is facing a terminal illness they could care less about the investment because their preference has shifted to focusing on health for their child.

The ego loves making a big deal over inconsequential things—how much money you make, how large your house or bank account is, how many letters there are behind your name, what is your title or position, etcetera. Yet none of these matters are particularly important when facing a challenge of faith or values. It is then that outer concerns lose relevance and your attention is converted back to your highest concerns. I have seen it happen many times. It amounts to a kind of spiritual balancing. You may have moved so far from your heart that life has to bring you back.

Disciplined meditation creates mental tenacity. Utilizing the processes in this book, enables you to fix your attention on the only thing that is forever and constant—the love and peace you hold within. The methods outlined supply the easy way back to wholeness.

The key is to stay centered in whatever is before you—this moment, this location, this event, this interaction. This mental training frees you to respond from a place of inner stillness—spiritual stability.

Nature offers a wonderful example of rhythm and flow. Nothing rushes in nature, yet everything is in constant motion. Observe the swaying of the trees, trickling of the brook, scurrying of animals, gentle falling of leaves, the ocean tide flowing in and out.

Can you sense the natural rhythm? Everything moves with rhythm. This grace and flow is your rhythm too. When you align with it, you begin to recognize an innate peacefulness. Moving into nature facilitates mental stillness and new, subtle, creative thoughts begin to emerge.

Peace cannot be obtained from an outside source. It must be experienced internally. Your Inner Source is ever ready to pour Its inspiration into your mind. Your job is to create the proper mental

VI. Meditation: The Antithesis of Anxiety

The more regularly and the more deeply you meditate, the sooner you will find yourself acting always from a center of peace.
J. Donald Walters

First: Move into Natural Rhythm

To a mind that is still. The whole universe surrenders.
Anonymous

We live in a world where every kind of technology and distraction is available. We can watch a rugby game in another country, talk on the phone, check emails, and balance the check book all at the same time and as we do this our attention is nowhere and everywhere and we are fragmented. Fragmentation leads to confusion and chaos. Struggle and anxiety result.

Managing the mind is the answer. You have within you a vast space of peace and a heart of kindness and compassion. Continuous focus on the outer world (watching the news, *checking in* with everyone, constant distraction) is a recipe for overwhelm. Devoting time to concentrate on inner stillness reverts the mind to natural calmness and inspiration. This can be accomplished through practiced concentration and focused breathing.

Scientists and academics have documented many positive effects of utilizing Eastern techniques, such as meditation. For instance, meditation is known to improve attention. Harvard neuroscientist Sara Lazar has shown that long-term meditators have thicker cortexes (the area of the brain that specializes in high-level decision making.) It has been well established that the cortex in general shrinks with age; however, Lazar found that the effects of regular meditation on the cortex was so profound that fifty-year-old meditators had a prefrontal cortex that looked like that of a twenty-five-year-old.

Even an eight-week class on mindfulness had a significant impact on the brain and stress-reduction. Subjects participating in a mindfulness program had smaller amygdalae—the aggressive part of the brain that reacts to stress. And a larger temporoparietal junctions (TPJs), the part of the brain associated with empathy and compassion.

It has been well established that Meditation and/or the practice of Tai Chi lowers blood pressure and enhances cognitive function. Similar findings are evident with the practice of Yoga. Additional research indicates that meditation changes the brain and lowers inflammation all the things you love to do and be sure to enjoy it thoroughly. (Eat ice cream for breakfast.) Lastly, choose to be around people who laugh. When they laugh, you laugh.

The saying is that the two hardest things to handle are failure and success. Both are more easily managed with humor. The happiest people don't necessarily have the most or best stuff. They just make the best of everything.

Whatever it is that you struggle with—an empty nest, an unfulfilling job, divorce, retirement or whatever, get busy. Reboot your perspective. Squash the struggle and you'll have a lot more energy to create the life you want. You know… whistle while you work (or walk), sing as you travel your road in life. My goodness, what if someone doesn't approve. Impossible! Laugh at the silliness of that notion. Goodness, if anyone deserves to relax and be himself, it would be you!